LAUGHTER
THE BEST MEDICINE™
@WORK

LAUGHTER
THE BEST MEDICINE™
@WORK

BANANACO PROFITS

America's Funniest
Jokes, Quotes,
and Cartoons

Reader's
Digest

The Reader's Digest Association, Inc.
New York, NY/Montreal

FOR READER'S DIGEST
Project Manager and Art Director: Elizabeth Tunnicliffe
Humor Editor, *Reader's Digest* Magazine: Andy Simmons
Senior Art Director: George McKeon
Editor-in-Chief, Books & Home Entertainment: Neil Wertheimer
Associate Publisher, Trade Publishing: Rosanne McManus
President and Publisher, Trade Publishing: Harold Clarke
Editor-in-Chief, Reader's Digest North America: Liz Vaccariello

Library of Congress Cataloging-in-Publication Data is available on request.

Cover and spot illustrations: George McKeon
Cartoon Credits: John Caldwell: *19, 29, 50, 58, 168;* Dave Carpenter: *24, 36, 89, 128, 157, 176;*
Joe di Chiarro: *61;* Roy Delgado: *99, 184, 200, 213;* Ralph Hagen: *11, 67, 106, 116, 163;*
Mike Lynch: *41, 55, 64;* Scott Arthur Masear: *6, 135, 144, 192;* Harley Schwadron: *103, 111, 139;*
Steve Smeltzer: *84, 92, 181, 205;* Thomas Bros.: *76, 81, 96, 197, 208;* Kim Warp: *70, 189;*
WestMach: *14, 151, 173*

We are committed to both the quality of our products and the service we provide to
our customers. We value your comments, so please feel free to contact us.

The Reader's Digest Association, Inc.
Adult Trade Publishing
44 S. Broadway
White Plains, NY 10601

For more Reader's Digest products and information, visit our website:

www.rd.com (in the United States)
www.readersdigest.ca (in Canada)

Printed in China

1 3 5 7 9 10 8 6 4 2

@@@@@@@@@@@@@@@@@@@@@@@@@@@@@@@@@@

A Note from the Editors

Bosses usually aren't very funny—at least not when it's *your* boss standing in front of your desk with eyes and mouth ablaze. But start telling boss jokes with your friends on a casual Saturday evening, and the laughter can shake the house.

Truth is, the workplace can be absurd, goofy, ridiculous, and sometimes, really fun. After all, there are so many opportunities for crazy things to be said and done—in job applications, meetings, speeches, customer complaints, and coffee breaks.

Reader's Digest has been sharing laughs about the work world in our magazine pages for decades. Now we've gathered the funniest of the funny into one volume. In the pages ahead you'll find hundreds of our most hilarious jokes, cartoons, and real-life experiences about all things work. You may wonder if someone *really* wrote that in their résumé, or said that in a meeting, or encountered such a customer in their store. Then you'll pause and say, "Sure!" because we've *all* witnessed something just like it.

What makes laughter the best medicine is its ability to erase stress, change negative moods to positive, and put the craziness of life into a bigger, happier perspective. All this is particularly true when it comes to work. So come Monday morning, when your boss is heading your way, keep these jokes in mind and smile. Because life is too short for anything else.

WORK DU SOLEIL

@@@@@@@@@@@@@@@@@@@@@@@@@@@@@@@

Contents

The Search

BANANACO PROFITS

"The closest to perfection a person ever comes is when he fills out a job application."

—KEN KRAFT

@@@@@@@@@@@@@@@@@@@@@@@@@@@@@@@@

Amusing Ads

A recent job posting on monster.com tells it like it really is: "Each new member of our team participates in eight weeks of management training classes done in on-site classrooms during the curse of the normal workday."

—SHERI JARMAN

Job ad in the York, PA., Daily Record: "Attention: Good hours, excellent pay, fun place to work, paid training, mean boss. Oh well, four out of five isn't bad."

During a recent job search, I encountered many well-meaning human resources personnel. Often, if a position was filled, they sent letters to the other candidates informing them that someone else had been chosen. One especially empathetic human-resources manager wrote, "I'm sorry to say that we were able to find a candidate who fits our requirements."

—JOAN M. WEIS

An ad in our church bulletin read: "Receptionist needed for busy chiropractic office." I faxed my resumé and got called for an interview. After hanging up, I realized I didn't know the name or location of the business. I found two listings for chiropractors in the phone book and dialed the first number. "Are you hiring a receptionist?" I asked politely.

"Why?" countered a cold-rasped voice. "Do I sound that bad?"

—JAYNE THURBER-SMITH

An employment website boasted that it provided training, counseling, and placement services. What's more, "many services are available in Spanish, and we arrange interrupters."

—CLARA EMLEN

@@@@@@@@@@@@@@@@@@@@@@@@@@@@@@@

@@@@@@@@@@@@@@@@@@@@@@@@@@@@@@@@@

Outside a California penitentiary: **"Now taking applications."**
—MALLORY PRITCHARD

Walking down the street, a dog saw a sign in an office window. "Help wanted. Must type 70 words a minute. Must be computer literate. Must be bilingual. An equal-opportunity employer."

The dog applied for the position, but was quickly rebuffed. "I can't hire a dog for the job," the office manager said. But when the dog pointed to the line that read "An equal-opportunity employer," the office manager sighed and asked, "Can you type?" Silently, the dog walked over to a typewriter and flawlessly banged out a letter. "Can you operate a computer?" the manager inquired. The dog then sat down at a terminal, wrote a program and ran it perfectly.

"Look, I still can't hire a dog for this position," said the exasperated office manager. "You have fine skills, but I need someone who's bilingual. It says so right in the ad."

The dog looked up at the manager and said, "Meow."
—LAWRENCE VAN GELDER

A job application made me do a double take. After the entry "Sex," the applicant had written, "Once in Florida."
—SUSAN WEBB

Looking over the job listings on The Home Depot website, I noticed one with a highly peculiar job description: "On rare occasions there may be a need to move or lift light articles. Examples include executive assistant, bank loan officer and accounting clerk."
—DENNIS E. BOWYER

Private school has a position open for science teacher. Must be certified or certifiable.
—VILMA COOK

@@@@@@@@@@@@@@@@@@@@@@@@@@@@@@@@

From The (Newark, New Jersey) Star-Ledger: "Auditions for Sly Fox, seeking nine men ages 20 to 90 and two women (one young and innocent, one not)."

—CHARLES COLLINS

I just saw an ad for a position I feel completely qualified for: "Wanted: bartenders. No exp. necessary. Must have: legal ID, phone, transportation, and teeth."

—AMY GOSS

I called a temp agency looking for work, and they asked if I had any phone skills. I said, "I called you, didn't I?"

—ZACH GALIFIANAKIS

Under "Help Wanted" in The North Missourian: "Chuck Anderson Ford-Mercury is looking for new and used salespeople."

—TYSON OTTO

The sign in the store window read: No Help Wanted. As two men passed by, one said to the other, "You should apply—you'd be great."

—E. M. UNGER

These inventive ads all appeared in a neighborhood newspaper in San Antonio, Texas.

- "Man, Honest. Will take anything."
- "Wanted: Chambermaid in rectory. Love in, $200 a month."
- "Wanted: Man to take care of cow that does not smoke or drink."
- "Tired of cleaning yourself? Let me do it."

—AUDREY POSELL

@@@@@@@@@@@@@@@@@@@@@@@@@@@@@

"Actually, what I need in an assistant is someone who knows how to work the cappucino machine."

On a sign in a fabric store: "Help Wanted. Must have knowledge of sewing, crafts and quitting."

Experienced cooks specializing in Italian cuisine & waitresses.

—R. BETTS

Help wanted ad in the Newport News, Va., Daily Press: "Satellite installers needed. Must have own transportation."

—WAVERLY TRAYLOR

@@@@@@@@@@@@@@@@@@@@@@@@@@@@@@@@@

On the door of a Virginia grocery store: **"Now hiring—two part-time perishable clerks."**

—BENTON TAYLOR

Here's a company that has low standards and doesn't mind owning up. Its help-wanted ad: "Seeking laborers, equipment operators, and dumb truck drivers."

—CAROLYN CHEATHAM

"Help wanted—local pallet-maker needs hardworking employees," read the ad in the Lebanon (Missouri) Daily Record. "Please do not apply if you oversleep, have no car, have no baby-sitter everyday, experience flat tires every week, leave early for probation meeting. Must be able to work and talk at same time."

—MARTINA EDWARDS

Ridiculous Résumés

An enthusiastic young woman came into the nursing home where I work, and filled out a job application. After she left, I read her form and had to admire her honesty. To the question "Why do you want to work here?" she had responded, "To get experience for a better job."

—DEBORAH L. BLAND

In the department store where I worked, my boss had asked me to look into hiring several cashiers. Reading through job applications, I burst out laughing at one answer. Next to the question "Salary expectations," the applicant had written a single word: "Yes."

—MICHEL PAYETTE

@@@@@@@@@@@@@@@@@@@@@@@@@@@@@@

I was updating my résumé and at the same time decided to update my husband's too. When I reached the "Postsecondary studies" on Marc's, I asked, "Honey, what were your minor and major when you did your Bachelor of Arts at the University of Ottawa?"

"I don't remember," he replied.

"Why don't you check on your diploma?" I suggested.

After a few moments, I heard him laughing. "There's a problem: I got my diploma printed in Latin, and I can't read it anymore."

—LISA LEVESQUE-DESROSIERS

Reviewing an employee's file in our human-resources office, I came across the information sheet he had completed when he was first hired. In the blank for whom we should contact in an emergency, he had filled in his girlfriend's name. Next to it was a blank for "relationship." He had written: "shaky."

—DONI FRAZIER

Recently, our 18-year-old daughter started hunting for her first real job. She spent an afternoon filling out application forms, leaving them on the kitchen table to finish later. As I walked by, a section of the application on top jumped out at me. Under "Previous Employment" she wrote, "Baby Sitting."

In answer to "Reason for Leaving," she replied, "Parents came home."

—DONALD GEISER

One of the less difficult blanks to fill in on our job-agency application is "Position Wanted."

One job seeker wrote **"Sitting."**

—FLO TRAYWICK

@@@@@@@@@@@@@@@@@@@@@@@@@@@@@@@@@

One read through this man's résumé and it was no wonder he was looking for a new line of work: Under "Previous Job," he'd written, **"Stalker at Walmart."**

—CINTHIA ALBERS

I stressed to my Grade XII class the need to present themselves positively in their letters of application for employment. One of my students took my words to heart. Instead of the customary "Yours Truly" or "Sincerely," he wrote "Eventually Yours."

—LESLIE M. WALKER

Despite years of exceeding quota in my sales career, my lack of education was an obstacle whenever I searched for work. Finally, I started listing under "education" on my résumé, "College of Hard Knocks."

I was surprised, then, to be hired as regional sales manager by a Fortune 500 company that had required a degree in its job posting. Soon after I started, my boss came by and asked me, "So what was your major at the University of Knoxville?"

—JOE BOSCH

Finding a job after prison is tough. Nevertheless, I refused to run from my past. So while filling out an application for a video wholesaler, I answered questions honestly. When it asked about previous employer, I wrote: Dept. of Corrections. Job description? Barber/inmate. Earnings? Fifty cents an hour. How long? Six years. Why did you leave? They let me. I got the job.

—PAUL DEGGES

I won't be hiring this assistant soon, even if her résumé boasts, "I'm a team player with 16 years of assassinating experience."

—CINDY DONALSON

@@@@@@@@@@@@@@@@@@@@@@@@@@@@@@

Looking for a job?

Be sure to proof your résumé and cover letters!

Dear Sir or Madam:

- "I am sure you have looked through several résumés with the same information about work experience, education, and references. I am not going to give you any of that stuff."

- "My mother delivered me without anesthesia, so I have an IQ of 146 and can therefore learn anything."

- "I enjoy working closely with customers, and my pleasant demeanor helps them feel comfortable and relaxed—not afraid."

- "I realize that my total lack of appropriate experience may concern those considering me for employment." But "I have integrity, so I will not steal office supplies and take them home."

- "In my next life, I will be a professional backup dancer or a rabbi," but for now, "I am attacking my résumé for you to review."

- "Thank you for your consideration. Hope to hear from you shorty!"

Sincerely, Hapless Job Seeker

—RESUMANIA.COM

The office where I work had received a number of résumés for a job opening. Although most of them were similar, one in particular stood out. In describing her current work responsibilities, a woman had written: "I conducted office affairs in the absence of the president."

—MARY SCHAFER

@@@@@@@@@@@@@@@@@@@@@@@@@@@@@@

"Ah, raised by wolves on the plains of Wyoming. And where did you learn about us?"

A résumé came across my desk at our software company. It was from a man clearly eager for a new line of work. Under the category "previous work experience," he'd written, "Peasant."

—M. L. HICKERSON

@@@@@@@@@@@@@@@@@@@@@@@@@@@@@@@@@

Résumé Bombs

- Candidate listed military service dating back to before he was born.

- Candidate claimed to be a member of the Kennedy family.

- Job seeker claimed to be the CEO of a company, when he was an hourly employee.

- Job seeker included samples of work, which were actually those of the interviewer.

- Candidate specified that his availability was limited because Friday, Saturday, and Sunday was "drinking time."

- A young man, whose one-line résumé showed a stint at a fast food restaurant, filled out our employment application, which consisted of three questions: "Why do you want to work here?" "What strengths would you bring to the company?" and "What did you dislike about your previous employment?"

  Skipping the first two, he answered the last question, "Pickles and onions."

—PAIGE SANDERSON

Catherine, a registered nurse, was unhappy with her job, so she submitted her resignation. She was sure she'd have no trouble finding a new position, because of the nursing shortage in her area. She e-mailed cover letters to dozens of potential employers and attached her résumé to each one. Two weeks later, Catherine was dismayed and bewildered that she had not received even one request for an interview.

Finally she received a message from a prospective employer that explained the reason she hadn't heard from anyone else. It read: "Your résumé was not attached as stated. I do, however, want to thank you for the vegetable lasagna recipe."

—HARRIET BROWN

@@@@@@@@@@@@@@@@@@@@@@@@@@@@@@@

Some people might object to filling out the part of our company's job application form that asks "Race."

Not one guy. He responded, **"Only on the interstate."**

—SARAH LONG

After being laid off, I papered the town with my résumé. Days passed and I hadn't received a single phone call, so I decided to take a closer look at the copies my husband had printed at his real estate office.

I quickly realized he hadn't put blank paper in the machine. At the bottom of each copy, written in bold, was a common real estate disclaimer: "The information contained herein, while deemed to be accurate, is not guaranteed."

—MARY CHISHOLM

Business executive to job hunter: "We're looking for people who can help make this company profitable again. I'll read your résumé for $200."

—RANDY GLASBERGEN

Done with running a home business, my wife decided to look for a staff job. One day when she was out, our phone rang. A woman asked for my wife and explained she was with an investor magazine. Because of my wife's business, we had gotten many solicitation calls for such periodicals. I quickly said, "She's not really interested in your magazine."

"That's odd," replied the woman, "because she just sent us her résumé."

—STEPHEN DUFRESNE

@@@@@@@@@@@@@@@@@@@@@@@@@@@@@@@@@@

Is there anything more likely to cause you an anxiety attack than your résumé getting stuck in the office copying maching?

—ORBEN'S CURRENT COMEDY

For a special season in my life, I had the pleasure of being a full-time "Mr. Mom."

During that time an acquaintance whom I hadn't seen for some time asked me what I did for a living. Sensitive to the question, I jokingly replied: "I'm the director of a residential unit, with primary responsibilities for the design and execution of life-style programs specifically targeted to a model family of four."

A week later I received a copy of his résumé in the mail.

—JAMES C. TANNER

An artist on Craigslist aimed this contest at potential employers: "Send me a week's worth of salary and benefits. I will keep and use it all. Whoever sends me the best salary package will win two days of graphic design work! Good luck.

Good luck! A college student applied for a summer job at a Welsh tourist attraction. But his e-mail address didn't help things. It was: atleastimnotwelsh.

—ANANOVA.COM

A human resources manager was going over one candidate's application. At the line saying, "Sign here," the woman had written, Pisces."

—JAMES DENT

 When does a hill become a mountain?
When it fills out an application for employment.

— MARILYN VOS SAVANT

@@@@@@@@@@@@@@@@@@@@@@@@@@@@@@@@@

Our 14-year-old son brought home an application for a job at a fast-food restaurant. When he asked me to check it over, I saw that where the form said, "In case of emergency, please call_____," he had written: "911."

—ANITA K. HANSEN

If You Really Don't Want the Job ...

Robert Half International, a worldwide specialized-staffing firm, collects résumé bloopers as a cautionary exercise. Some favorites:

- "I demand a salary commiserate with my experience."

- "It's best for employers that I not work with people."

- "I have an excellent track record, although I am not a horse."

- "You will want me to be Head Honcho in no time."

- "Let's meet, so you can 'ooh' and 'aah' over my experience."

- "My goal is to be a meteorologist. But since I possess no training in meteorology, I suppose I should try stock brokerage."

- "References: None. I've left a path of destruction behind me."

- "Instrumental in ruining entire operation for a Midwest chain store."

- "Note: Please don't misconstrue my 14 jobs as 'job-hopping.' I have never quit a job."

—ANNE FISHER

I had prepared my son's résumé for a job application. I typed curriculum vitae at the top and his name underneath. He delivered the document to the company, and a week or so later, a letter came for him. The salutation read: "Dear Mr. Vitae."

—SHELAGH PRYKE

@@@@@@@@@@@@@@@@@@@@@@@@@@@@@@

"Once they noticed your tail wagging, they stopped upping their offer."

One of the more enjoyable aspects of my teacher-librarian job is reading through letters from children applying for the prestigious job of library monitor.

I had announced that applications should be addressed to "Mrs. Slattery" but the first two I opened lost all chance of success. One read: "Dear Mrs. Slavery" and the other "Dear Mrs. Fattery."

—ANNE SLATTERY

@@@@@@@@@@@@@@@@@@@@@@@@@@@@@@@@

Typos and grammatical errors are the most common mistakes creative professionals make on their résumés, according to a survey for *The Creative Group*. So if you're job-hunting, these examples of résumé gaffes should prove that two eyes are better than one spell-checker:

- "Languages: English and Spinach."
- "I was the company's liaison with the sock exchange."
- "I prefer a fast-paste work environment."
- "I'm attacking my résumé for you to review."
- "My work ethics are impeachable."

Having established a successful career as an architect, my uncle decided to change directions and pursue his dream of becoming a chef. After spending several years preparing elegant meals in restaurants and hotels, however, the unusual hours and low pay convinced him to return to his original profession.

He submitted résumé after résumé, and by the time he came across an ad for a Renaissance architect, his finances were running low. His cover letter obviously caught the attention of the prospective employer: "Though I don't have a wealth of experience in the area of Renaissance design, I am hoping that you will consider me for this job, because I am Baroque." He started work the following week.

—MELODY MCGRATH

A young man went to a Homosassa, Fla., hardware store looking for work but allegedly ended up stealing two hanguns and a watch. Police say he wasn't hard to find: he left his job application on the gun case.

@@@@@@@@@@@@@@@@@@@@@@@@@@@@@@@

The toughest part of applying for a new job is having to explain why you're no longer at your previous one. Here are rationalizations from cover letters that did no one any good:

- "My boss thought I could do better elsewhere."

- "The company made me a scapegoat, just like my three previous employers."

- "Responsibilities make me nervous."

—CHLOE RHODES, *THE OFFICE BOOK*, READER'S DIGEST BOOKS

A friend of my son had graduated and was looking for work. One day he saw his dream job advertised. He went to send his résumé, but could not find an envelope at first Finally he managed to find one under a pile of papers. He stuffed the letter inside and posted it.

Two weeks later he received a reply. Unfortunately, he was not being considered for the job. The company also returned a photo which had been in the envelope. Then he understood why his application had been turned down. It was a photo of him— much worse for wear, half-naked and being supported by two girls—taken at his graduation party!

—H. SCHEFFERS-VIS

Sending my résumé off in reply to a job advertisement, I thought my wealth of experience said it all. So instead of including a cover letter, I simply enclosed a note saying, "Dear Sir, I apply."
The reply was equally short: **"Dear Sir, we regret."**

—PAUL LANDSBERGER

@@@@@@@@@@@@@@@@@@@@@@@@@@@@@@@

I stopped working for three years to care for my two daughters. When I decided to go back to work, there was a "gap" on my résumé, which was not well received by potential employers. When I interviewed for a secretarial position, I solved the problem in a special way: I added three years experience in "Management and Production." Impressed, the interviewer asked me where it was that I worked.

"I managed my home and produced two daughters," I replied. I got the job!

—ADALGISA TEIXEIRA PETUCCO

Incredible Interviews

A friend and I used to run a small temporary-staffing service. Our agency did mandatory background checks on all job candidates, even though our application form asked them if they'd ever been convicted of a crime.

One day after a round of interviews, my coworker was entering information from a young man's application into the computer. She called me over to show me that he had noted a previous conviction for second-degree manslaughter. Below that, on the line listing his skills, he had written "Good with people."

—JANA RAHRIG

When my husband was interviewing job candidates, one of his standard questions was "What are your strengths?" He received a thank-you letter from one especially nervous young man in which the fellow wrote, "There's something I'd like to mention that completely slipped my mind during the interview. One of my biggest strong points is my excellent memory."

—MITA MUKHOPADHYAY

@@@@@@@@@@@@@@@@@@@@@@@@@@@@@@@@

Personnel officer to job candidate: "I notice you refer to your work history as a 'terrifying chain of events.'"

—COTHAM IN *THE WALL STREET JOURNAL*

I was interviewing a young woman who had applied for a job in our gift shop. It turned out that her favorite sport was soccer, and she was bending my ear about her accomplishments in the neighborhood league. Trying to steer the interview back to her job qualifications, I asked, "So, tell me about your long-range goals."

After thinking a minute, she replied, "Once I kicked the ball in from midfield."

—RALPH J. STEINITZ

Interviewing a candidate for a position in a tire factory, I noticed his hobbies included playing in a pop group. The job involved operating a computer and so one of the interview panel asked the candidate if he had any keyboard experience.

"No," he answered, "but I can sing, and we have a girl who plays piano."

—PAUL CONSTERDINE

An accountant answered an advertisement for a top job with a large firm. At the end of the interview, the chairman said, "One last question—what is three times seven?"

The accountant thought for a minute and replied, "Twenty-two."

Outside he took out his calculator and saw he should have said 21. He concluded he had lost the job. Two weeks later, however, he was offered the post. After a few weeks he asked the chairman why he had been appointed when he had given the wrong answer.

"You were the closest," the chairman replied.

—S. NETTLE

"The pay is great, but the commute is ridiculous."

For her summer job, my 18-year-old daughter arranged interviews at several day-care centers. At one meeting, she sat down on one of the kiddie seats, no simple task for most people. The interview went well, and at the end, the day-care center director asked the standard question, "Can you give me one good reason we should hire you?"

"Because I fit in the chairs." She got the job.

—JUDITH L. MCKAY

@@@@@@@@@@@@@@@@@@@@@@@@@@@@@@@@

Going on a job interview?

Take pity on the poor hiring managers, who filed these reports:

- "The applicant smelled his armpits on the way to the interview room."

- "The candidate told the interviewer he was fired from his last job for beating up his boss."

- "An applicant said she was a 'people person,' not a 'numbers person,' in her interview for an accounting position."

—CAREERBUILDER.COM

Mac and Todd, two brothers, went together to an employment agency looking for work. The first brother was called for an interview. "It says here you're a pilot," said the employment counselor. Mac nodded. "Well, that's great. There's a need for experienced pilots. I have a job for you immediately." With that, Mac left for the airfield.

Todd's interview didn't go as well. When asked about his work experience, he replied, "I'm a tree cutter." The counselor said there were no openings for tree cutters. Incensed, Todd demanded: "How come you have a job for my brother and not for me?"

"Because your brother is a pilot," explained the counselor. "He has a specialized skill."

"What do you mean specialized? I cut the wood, and he piles it!"

—E. S. M.

When our daughter's boyfriend was preparing for a job interview, he balked at having to dress up. "It's a casual office," he argued. "Why should I show up in a suit and tie?"

Our daughter Heather smiled and told him, "You have to make the team before you get to wear the uniform."

—DOROTHY DAVIS

QUOTABLE QUOTES

"Never wear a backward baseball cap to an interview unless applying for the job of umpire."

—DAN ZEVIN

"When you go in for a job interview, I think a good thing to ask is if they ever press charges."

—JACK HANDY

"Oh, you hate your job? Why didn't you say so? There's a support group for that. It's called EVERYBODY, and they meet at the bar."

—DREW CAREY

"If you call failures experiments, you can put them in your résumé and claim them as achievements."

—MASON COOLEY

"Résumé: A written exaggeration of only the good things a person has done in the past, as well as a wish list of the qualities a person would like to have."

—BO BENNETT

"A lot of people quit looking for work as soon as they find a job."

—ZIG ZIGLAR

"Experience is not what happens to a man. It is what a man does with what happens to him."

—ALDOUS HUXLEY

"Beware of all enterprises that require new clothes."

—HENRY DAVID THOREAU

"Never take a job where winter winds can blow up your pants."

—GERALDO RIVERA

@@@@@@@@@@@@@@@@@@@@@@@@@@@@@@@

A job applicant was asked, "What would you consider to be your main strengths and weaknesses?"

"Well," he began, "my main weakness would definitely be my issues with reality—telling what's real from what's not."

"Okay," said the interviewer. "And what are your strengths?"

"I'm Batman."

Our friend Alex emigrated from Russia to the United States and was looking for a job in engineering. During one interview the personnel director remarked how difficult it was to pronounce typically long Russian names. "What?" Alex said. "And you think Massachusetts is easy?

—MARION H. MAIDENS

Running late for a job interview at a large men's fashion company, I grabbed a white dress shirt that I didn't have time to iron.

The interview went well—until the end. "Just a word of advice," said my interviewer. "You might want to iron your shirt before your next job interview."

I held up the back of my shirt collar, revealing the tag. On it was the name of that very clothing company and the words wrinkle free.

I got the job.

—ANDREW COHEN

@@@@@@@@@@@@@@@@@@@@@@@@@@@@@@

I had to fill a position at our company's warehouse and decided to take a chance on a very eager—but inexperienced—applicant. Happily Joe did well and was soon ready to be trained on the forklift. The day he started, however, I heard the scrunch of metal meeting wood, followed by the piercing sound of an alarm system. I ran over and saw that the lift's forks had been driven through the shipping bay door, severing the alarm contacts.

"Joe, what happened?" I asked, gaping at the damage.

"Well," he said sheepishly. "Did I mention that I can't drive?"

—SYLVIA SUMMERS

An electrician is interviewing for a construction job.

"Can you roll your hard hat down your arm and make it pop back on your head?" the supervisor asks.

"Sure," he replies, confused.

"Can you bounce your screwdriver off the concrete, spin in a circle and catch it in your tool pouch?"

"Yes, sir," he answers excitedly.

"And can you quick-draw your wire stripper, twirl it and slip it into your pouch like it's a holster?"

"I've been doing that for years!"

"In that case, I can't use you," the boss says. "I've got 15 guys doing that now."

—KENNETH CROUCH

"I'm tired of begging people for money," a man said to an employment counselor. "Can you help me find a job?"

"How long have you been out of work?" the counselor asked.

"Who said anything about not having a job?" the man replied. **"I work for PBS."**

—JAMES R. WILKES

@@@@@@@@@@@@@@@@@@@@@@@@@@@@@@

My sister Angela was impressed by a job applicant's confidence. "How will you gain your coworkers' respect?" she asked. The reply: **"Mainly through my misdemeanor."**

—GRETCHEN DUFF

So When Do I Start?

How do you get human resources to remember you? Try pulling some of these actual interview stunts.

- Balding applicant abruptly excused himself and returned a few minutes later wearing a hairpiece.

- Applicant asked to see the reviewer's résumé to see if the personnel executive was qualified to interview him.

- Applicant phoned his therapist during the interview for advice on answering specific questions.

- During the interview, an alarm clock went off in the applicant's briefcase. He apologized and said he had to leave for another interview.

- Applicant challenged the interviewer to arm-wrestle.

—GRADVIEW.COM

One applicant for a job at my print shop stood out from the rest. He was clean-cut, well-mannered and during his interview addressed me as "Sir." I discovered why when I looked over his written application.

In response to the question about military service, he had written "yes." Then he added, "It started when I was 11 and my new stepdad turned out to be an ex-Marine drill sergeant."

—PATRICK N. MCKENZIE

@@@@@@@@@@@@@@@@@@@@@@@@@@@@@@@

Our teenage grandson was eager to get his first summer job working for a bicycle rental shop. During his interview he was asked, "How are you at handling irate customers?"

"I haven't had experience with irate customers," he replied, "but I'm pretty good with irate parents."

He got the job.

—ANNE CURTIS

When we moved from Virginia to Oregon, I applied for the position of animal-control officer with the local police department. The selection process required an in-depth investigation of my past, including contacting employees at the animal shelter in Virginia where I had worked. During the final interview, the investigating officer told me that he had received some nice comments about me. Then, with a laugh, he shared a particularly memorable remark. When asked if I had any prejudices, a former colleague replied, "I don't think she likes cocker spaniels very much."

I got the job anyway.

—SUZANNE L. PILON

A man walked into a Taco Bell in Haverstraw, New York, and pulled a gun on the cashier. After grabbing the loot, he marched into the manager's office and applied for a job. He was turned down.

—LOHUD.COM

After taking early retirement, I attended an interview for the role of litter warden at the local park.

"What training do I get?" I asked the council official.

"None," he shrugged. "You just pick it up as you go along."

—KEITH HAMBER

@@@@@@@@@@@@@@@@@@@@@@@@@@@@@@

"Our consultant recommended this temporary title until the staff gets to know you."

I had an interview for a job in a library and I asked my brother for advice.

"Just talk quietly," he said.

—CHARLOTTE JOSEPH

@@@@@@@@@@@@@@@@@@@@@@@@@@@@@@@@

Rajesh is at an interview for a guard's job. "Assume you see two trains speeding towards each other. What will you do?" asked a Railways official.

"Raise a red flag," Rajesh replied.

"But you haven't taken the flag with you,"said the official.

"I'll wave my red shirt at the drivers."

"You're not wearing a red shirt that day."

"Then I'll run home and bring my little sister," Rajesh smiled.

"Wow! Does she know any new technique?"

"No," said Rajesh. "But she hasn't seen two trains collinding."

"I see you were last employed by a psychiatrist," said the employer to the applicant. "Why did you leave?"

"Well," the applicant replied, "I just couldn't win. If I was late to work, I was hostile. If I was early, I had an anxiety complex, and if I was on time, I was compulsive."

—CAO XIN

Don't Call Us

Recruitment website CareerBuilder.com surveyed employers to find some of the biggest job-interview gaffes from the last year:

- Candidate who answered mobile phone and asked the interviewer to leave her own office, because it was a "private" conversation.

- Candidate who asked the interviewer for a lift home.

- Candidate who, when offered food, declined, saying he didn't want to line his stomach with grease before going out drinking.

- Candidate who flushed the toilet while talking to employer during a phone interview.

@@@@@@@@@@@@@@@@@@@@@@@@@@@@@@@@@@

We'll Call You

Remember, the idea behind job interviews is to make an impression—a good one, say these hiring executives.

- "One candidate said that we should hire him because he would be a great addition to our softball team."

- "An applicant sang all her responses to interview questions."

- "One individual said we had nice benefits, which was good because he was going to need to take a lot of leave the following year."

- "A candidate told me she needed the position because she wanted to get away from dealing with people."

—ACCOUNTEMPS

A friend of mine who is manager for advertising in a fashion magazine was interviewing applicants for the job of manager of advertising sales. One of the applicants seemed ideal for the job. My friend resolved silently to hire this girl, and asked her the final question: What do you think of our magazine?"

"It's an excellent publication," answered the interviewee, "but there are too many ads in it."

—MARIA PETROVA

Bob had applied for a job in a supermarket and was attending the interview. When the interviewer asked what experience he'd had, Bob said that he'd once worked in another supermarket.

The interviewer asked why he had left.

"I was sacked for playing with the bacon slicer," Bob explained.

The interviewer was puzzled: "Surely they didn't consider that to be a serious offence?"

"They must have," replied Bob. "They sacked her too."

—ADAM CUTHBERTSON

@@@@@@@@@@@@@@@@@@@@@@@@@@@@@@@@@@

When I went for my first student-job interview at a supermarket, some friends advised me on a technique that would impress the manager. I was told to smile frequently and use the word "sir."

Unfortunately, the ploy didn't work. The more I smiled and said "sir," the grimmer my interviewer became. My interview ended when the boss suddenly stood up and showed me the door.

"Don't call us," she said coldly, smoothing down her skirt. "We'll call you."

—FRANCES WHITESTONE

Nervous during an interview for his first part-time job, my 15-year-old son tried to answer each question as honestly as he could. When he was asked to explain his strengths, he thought a moment, then offered, "Well, I can bench press 100 pounds."

—JOY GALLANT

While my wife was getting a haircut, a young man wearing jeans and a T-shirt walked in, seeking a job. After the applicant left, my wife's stylist, sporting multiple earrings, a nose ring and bright blue hair, said, "Can you believe someone would come in and ask for a job dressed like that?"

—JOHN GRATTON

A police officer was interviewing a young recruit. "If you're driving on a lonely road at night," the officer asked, "and you're being chased by a gang of criminals going 60 m.p.h., what would you do?"

The applicant replied, **"Seventy!"**

—DAVID BROOME

@@@@@@@@@@@@@@@@@@@@@@@@@@@@@@@@@

Interviewer to job applicant: **"Can you come up with any reason you want this job other than your parents want you out of their house?"**

—MIKE SHAPIRO

Two friends go to a job interview. The first one goes in and is asked by the interviewer, "Tell me, when you look at me, what is the first thing you see?"

"Well," he answers, "that you have no ears."

"How dare you! Get out!" the interviewer demands.

He leaves and warns his friend, "Don't mention that he has no ears it apparently annoys him."

"Thank you," says the friend.

So the second interviewee is asked the same question when he enters the office: "Tell me, when you look at me, what is the first thing you see?"

"I see that you wear contact lenses," answers the second friend.

"Excellent!" exclaims the interviewer, "how did you know?"

"Simple, where would you rest your glasses if you didn't?"

—ILEANA CONTERNO

My daughter Miranda works in a lingerie shop, and one evening a young man came in and asked for a job application. After he asked a few questions, Miranda explained the rules for male employees. "You can only work behind the cash register or in the stockroom," she said. "You can't wait on customers, or go into the changing areas.

"By the way," she added, "most of our customers don't look like the models in the ads, but more like your mother."

With that, the young man tossed the application on the counter and walked out the door.

—SCOTT SWANN

@@@@@@@@@@@@@@@@@@@@@@@@@@@@@@

A job applicant's polygraph test for the Washington State
Patrol came to an abrupt end after officers discovered an
interesting piece of literature on the front seat of his car. The title
of the book: How to Beat a Lie Detector Test.

—KOMONEWS.COM

I'm in personnel with the government in Washington, D.C.,
reviewing applications for federal employment. The standard
form includes the question "Why did you leave your previous
employment?" One applicant, a former U.S. Congressman,
responded, "The express wish of 116,000 voters."

—WILSON M. CARR III

**"Obviously, we were thinking long term when
we assembled this board."**

@@@@@@@@@@@@@@@@@@@@@@@@@@@@@@@

I attached great importance to dressing well for job interviews. At one interview, when I noticed that the employers and other applicants were looking at me intently, I assumed they were all struck by my tidy appearance.

I got the job. However, one interviewer took me aside and said: "We chose you because you looked natural, even though you had tissue paper stuck to your forehead."

—SUPREEYA PROMTHONG

I joined a company's Human Resources department after graduating from college. In just a few years, I was promoted to be the senior officer responsible for recruiting junior and mid-level clerks. I was only 25, and most of the applicants were older than me. To impress these applicants at the interviews, I dressed and talked quite maturely.

One day, a woman in her forties applied for a clerical job. At the interview she complained that it was hard to find work since older women were discriminated against.

"That's really unfair," I tried to console her, "plus you look much younger than your age."

She smiled instantly and said politely, "Don't worry, you look very young as well."

—C. L. WONG

In an interview, a plastic surgeon was asked if he'd ever done anything shocking.

"I don't think so," he replied. **"But I've certainly raised a few eyebrows."**

—P. BACANIN

@@@@@@@@@@@@@@@@@@@@@@@@@@@@@@@@

To check the character of the prospective department
head, the boss says: "Let's assume you go to my
house and ring the doorbell. My wife invites you in,
but tells you that I won't be home for another two hours.
What would you do?"

The applicant hesitates, then asks,
"Could you let me see a photo of your wife?"

—LEA BERNER

As a foreman for a construction company, my friend Jim was
interviewing an applicant. He asked the plasterer to bring his
tools in so he could see what he could do. The fellow returned
with tools slung over his shoulder and hanging from his pockets,
and in one hand he was holding an unidentifiable object covered
in plaster. Jim asked what it was. "My radio," the chap answered.

"All right," said Jim, "you can start tomorrow."

The applicant looked surprised. "That's it? You don't want to
see what I can do?"

"Any plasterman who has a radio looking like that one," Jim
said, "must have put in at least three years of work."

—JENNIFER MARCOUX

I agreed when my 17-year-old niece asked me if she could
use my name as a reference on her résumé, which she planned
to submit to a local fast-food restaurant. A few days later she
called and asked me if I could meet her at the restaurant later that
afternoon. "Yes, but why?" I asked.

"The manager wants me to come in for an interview," she
explained, "and she wants me to bring my references."

—JOYCE SCHWAB

@@@@@@@@@@@@@@@@@@@@@@@@@@@@@@@@

Armed with impeccable credentials, a man applied for a position with a top company. Unfortunately, he had a problem with one of his eyes—it constantly winked. "We'd love to hire you," said the company vice president, "but that winking is too distracting."

"Wait! I can make it stop by taking two aspirin," the applicant said.

"Okay, show me," the executive replied.

The job candidate reached into his pocket, pulled out a dozen condom packages and placed them on the desk before finding two aspirin. He took the tablets, and the winking stopped.

"That's fine," the VP said coolly. "But we don't condone womanizing."

"No, no. You've got me all wrong," the man replied. "Have you ever asked for aspirin at the drugstore while winking?"

—DAN GUERRA

Sales manager to an applicant: "Have you any previous sales experience?"

"Yes, sir. I sold my house, my car, the piano and almost all my wife's jewelry."

Here's a job to avoid: hiring manager.

See what you'd have to contend with?

- The candidate told the interviewer he wouldn't stay with the job long because he might get an inheritance if his uncle died— and the old man wasn't "looking too good."

- The candidate said she couldn't provide a writing sample because all her writing had been for the CIA and it was "classified."

—CAREERBUILDER.COM

@@@@@@@@@@@@@@@@@@@@@@@@@@@@@@@

The employer addressed the applicant: "We want a responsible person for this job."

"Then I'm your man," announced the young man. **"No matter where I've worked, whenever anything happened, they always said I was responsible."**

—JEAN BULL

All my self-confidence and poise vanished as I entered the office for a job interview. As I closed the door behind me, the woman behind the desk in the farthest corner of the room commanded, "Sit down!"

I sat in the nearest chair by the door. With a puzzled look, she stood up, her hand extended. However, before I reached her, she again barked, "Sit!".

I sat in the chair by her desk for a second before I jumped up to grasp her still-outstretched hand. Our greeting was interrupted by yet another "Sit!".

I yo-yoed, still clutching her hand, back to the chair. After I was hired, I was assured it was because of my qualifications and not because I was more obedient than her dog.

—JAN JOHNSON

Many people have been trained in interview techniques, but not my 19-year-old nephew from Amsterdam. He had applied for a job as crane operator and had an interview. He knew that, besides him, there was only one other candidate. During the interview he was asked: "Why should we employ you?"

"How should I know?" my nephew answered. "I've never met the other guy!"

—KITTY APPELMAN

@@@@@@@@@@@@@@@@@@@@@@@@@@@@@@

Employer to job candidate: **"I hire only married people.
They're less likely to go home early."**

—HARLEY SCHWADRON

My buddy applied for a job as an insurance salesperson.
Where the form requested "prior experience," he wrote
"lifeguard." That was it. Nothing else.

"We're looking for someone who can not only sell insurance,
but who can sell himself," said the hiring manager. "How does
working as a lifeguard pertain to salesmanship?"

"I couldn't swim," my pal replied.

He got the job.

—TEDD C. HUSTON

Interview Impact

*When you're interviewing for a job, you want to make an impression.
Hiring managers report that these people made one—just not the
right kind:*

- Applicant hugged hiring manager at the end of the interview.

- Applicant ate all the candy from the candy bowl while trying to
answer questions.

- Applicant blew her nose and lined up the used tissues on the
table in front of her.

- Applicant wore a hat that said "Take this job and shove it."

- Applicant talked about how an affair cost him a previous job.

- Applicant threw his beer can in the outside trashcan before
coming into the reception area.

- Applicant's friend came in and asked, "How much longer?"

—CAREERBUILDER.COM

@@@@@@@@@@@@@@@@@@@@@@@@@@@@@@@@

A personnel manager was interviewing an applicant for a job with his company. "How long did you work in your previous position?"

"Fifty-five years," replied the applicant.

"And how old are you?" asked the manager, clearly shocked at the applicant's answer.

"I'm 47," said the applicant.

"I'm sorry," relied the manager, "I don't understand."

"It's simple," smiled the applicant. "Overtime."

—SHEHERYAR HAFEEZ

My husband, a tool shop manager, was in charge of interviewing applicants for a new store opening in our town. Two young brothers from the country entered his office looking for work. At the end of the interview, my husband asked them to bring him photographs for their records. Early the next day the two brothers brought in an enormous photo of the two of them, smiling and hugging each other!

—RENATA BERNARDO

In search of a new pastor, our congregation advertised for someone "able to walk on water and move mountains." We knew we had the right person when a candidate arrived for the job interview sporting a life jacket and carrying a shovel.

—MARJORIE KAUFMAN

A man saw a job advertised as 'Problem Solver' with a salary of $100,000. He applied, had an interview and was offered the job on the spot. "Do you have any questions?" asked his new employer.

"Just one," replied the man. "How can you afford to pay so much?"

"That," said the employer, "is your first problem."

—COLIN JAMES

@@@@@@@@@@@@@@@@@@@@@@@@@@@@@@@@@

The boss asked four job applicants the same question: "What is two and two?"

The first interviewee was a journalist. His answer was "twenty-two." The second, an engineer, calculated the answer to be between 3.999 and 4.001. The third applicant, a lawyer, cited a court case in which two and two was proved to be four.

The last candidate was an accountant. When the accountant heard the question, he leaned across the desk and said in a low voice, "How much do you want it to be?"

After many years of staying home to raise a family, my mother was nervous about her job interview for the position of librarian at our high school.

During the interview the principal asked her if she read. Since six children didn't leave her much spare time, she reluctantly admitted, "No." However, thinking this might hinder her chances, she quickly added, "But I can!" She got the job.

—ANNETTE GALLANT

On the Job

BANANACO PROFITS

"Don't stay in bed, unless you can make money in bed.

—GEORGE BURNS

"Dawson takes a lot of work home with him. But he never seems to bring it back."

@@@@@@@@@@@@@@@@@@@@@@@@@@@@@@@@

Corporate Miscommunications

The company where I work provides four-foot-high cubicles so each employee can have some privacy. One day a coworker had an exasperating phone conversation with one of her teenage sons. After hanging up, she heaved a sigh and said, "No one ever listens to me."

Immediately, several voices from surrounding cubicles called out, "Yes, we do."

—JO JAIMESON

At our supermarket, I noticed a woman with four boys and a baby. Her patience was wearing thin as the boys called out, "Mommy! Mommy!" while she tried to shop. Finally, she blurted out, "I don't want to hear the word mommy for at least ten minutes!"

The boys fell silent for a few seconds. Then one tugged on his mother's dress and said softly, "Excuse me, miss."

—DENNIS DOOK

One day a coworker noticed I had on a new dress. She raved about how beautiful it was and wanted to know where I bought it. I told her the name of the store and jokingly added that if she ended up buying the same dress, she'd have to tell me when she was going to wear it so we didn't show up at the office looking like twins. She replied, "Oh, I'd never wear a dress like that to work!"

—NANCY J. HIMBER

My colleagues and I recently received this e-mail from the facilities department: "Due to construction, your office may be either cooler or warmer than usual on Tuesday. Dress accordingly."

—DEBRA DONATH

@@@@@@@@@@@@@@@@@@@@@@@@@@@@@@@@

Found on the bottom of an office memo:
"If you have any questions, please read again."

—STAN GLEASON

The topic in the office break room was the high price of divorce.

"I should've taken out a home improvement loan to pay for my attorney," said one disgusted woman.

"Can you do that?" I wondered.

"She got her bum husband out of the house, didn't she?" said a friend. "I'd call that a home improvement."

—MARTI MCDANIEL

The employee refrigerator at the graphic-design office where I work is notoriously messy. But I realized things were really getting out of hand when I saw an old jar of Vlasic-brand pickles that sported a new, handwritten label: Jurassic Pickles.

—HOLLY SPRINGER

The Employee/English Dictionary

- **Plutoed:** To be unceremoniously relegated to a lower position without an adequate explanation.

- **Clockroaches:** Employees who spend most of their day watching the clock instead of doing their jobs.

- **Prairie Dogging:** Occurs when workers simultaneously pop their heads up out of their cubicles to see what's going on.

- **Carbon-Based Error:** Error caused by a human, not a computer.

- **Bobbleheading:** The mass nod of agreement during a meeting to comments made by the boss.

—FROM *THE BUZZWORD DICTIONARY* BY JOHN WALSTON (MARION STREET PRESS, INC.)

A "safety message" sent out at my office warned: "Alert! The stress balls distributed at yesterday's 'How to Manage Your Stress' class are exploding all over the building. Please do not squeeze or apply pressure to the stress balls!"

—APRIL RICHEY

To be perfectly blunt, our office receptionist could be a real witch. She'd been there 20 years and lorded over the place like she owned it. One recent, freezing day, she went so far as to order a coworker to warm up her car for her. Much to my surprise, he agreed.

A few minutes later he came back holding a broom. Placing it on a heating vent, he told her, "Just give it a minute and it'll be ready to go."

—JESSICA O'NEILL

One morning at our small-town newspaper office, one of the editors was struggling to write a headline for the obituary of a woman who was noted for little besides a fondness for crossword puzzles. "What am I supposed to write," the editor whined, "'She liked puzzles'?"

Just then one of our copy editors piped up, "How about, 'Crossword fan is now six down'?"

—JAMES VLAHOS

A coworker stormed into my friend's office, yelling, "Did you tell Joan I was a witch?"

Stunned, my friend sputtered, **"No! I don't know how she found out."**

—GEORGE O'BRIEN

@@@@@@@@@@@@@@@@@@@@@@@@@@@@@@@

An executive for a phone company, my father often rode his motorcycle to the office from his suburban home. He wore coveralls over his clothing for protection, and would hang them on his clothes tree when he arrived at work. Once when he was working late, my mother called the office. His secretary answered the call. "He's not in his office," she told my mother.

"Has he left for the day?" my mother pressed.

"Oh, no," said the secretary. "He hasn't left the building—his pants are still on the clothes rack."

—WILLIAM B. MAGRUDER

I work in a small government office, and as part of the daily routine I take orders for doughnuts and pick them up on my midmorning run to the post office. A new employee looked bemused as I took orders for CCRs, GOFs and POFs—known to bakery staff as chocolate-covered raised, glazed old-fashioned and plain old-fashioned. When it was the new employee's turn to order, she laughed and said, "You know you work in a government office when even the doughnuts have acronyms."

—CINDY BEVING

Things you'll seldom hear around the office water cooler:

- "I love my boss so much I'd gladly work for free."

- "I'm going to run down to the cafeteria and ask the cook for his recipes."

- "Boy, I wish I could make coffee as good as that vending machine on the third floor."

- "I don't want the promotion if it's going to make my coworkers envious."

—*EXECUTIVE SPEECHWRITER NEWSLETTER*

My coworker is Venezuelan and has trouble understanding some English phrases. She is a top salesperson in our company and is known for being very competitive. One day she was talking with a couple of employees, complaining about her job and how she felt mistreated.

"Oh, be quiet," said a colleague. "You know you're queen bee at the office."

"Oh, really?" she replied indignantly. "And who is Queen A?"

—DENISE MADDOX

A woman and her daughter had just purchased a $1200 Persian rug at the store where I work. As they were leaving, I overheard the daughter say to her mother, "There's no way that we can tell Dad we've always had this."

—MATTHEW LARSON

"Harding is very security conscious."

@@@@@@@@@@@@@@@@@@@@@@@@@@@@@@

Our company was conducting free body mass index checkups. When a stout colleague climbed onto the machine, it spit out a slip of paper telling him what his weight-to-height ratio was and what it ought to be.

"What does it say?" I asked.

He replied, **"I need to increase my height by six inches."**

—SOBBY KURIAN

I work for an accounting firm where it's not unusual to have an IRS agent in the office examining taxpayer records. We try to let clients know when an agent is present so they will watch what they say.

One time a coworker handed a client a note that read "There is an IRS agent in the office." The client scribbled a response and handed it back to the accountant. "I know," the client wrote. "It's my brother-in-law."

—KATHY BIGLER

As an editor of the St. Louis Globe-Democrat, I received many unwanted phone calls. My secretary was exceptionally gracious in screening callers and saving me from pests.

One day I was talking with Howard F. Baer, a distinguished civic leader and chairman of the St. Louis Zoological Commission, when my wife called on another line.

"I'm sorry, but he's talking to Mr. Baer at the zoo," my secretary said.

"Really, Florence," my wife said, "you need a better story than that."

—MARTIN LAWLER DUGGAN

@@@@@@@@@@@@@@@@@@@@@@@@@@@@@

During a routine companywide drug screening, a coworker was sent into the bathroom with a plastic cup, while the attendant dutifully stood guard outside.

She waited patiently for several minutes. More time went by, until finally she knocked on the door.

"Are you all right in there?"

From within, a timid voice responded, "Don't I at least get a magazine or something?"

"No," said the nurse, without blinking. "It's not that kind of test."

—MARTY GUFFIN

I work at an aviation school that specializes in five-day refresher courses for aircraft mechanics. One day, I overheard a coworker talking on the phone with a potential customer. "Actually, we don't call our classes crash courses," he said. "We like to think of them as 'keep up in the air' classes."

—RANDY G. SMITH

Who Took My Stapler?

Is your cubicle neighbor driving you nuts? You're not alone. Here are just some of the ways coworkers annoy each other, in your own words:

- "Employee eats all the good cookies."
- "Employee's body is magnetic and keeps deactivating my access card."
- "Employee's aura is wrong."
- "Employee is too suntanned."
- "Employee smells like road ramps."
- "Employee wants to check a coworker for ticks."

—CAREERBUILDER.COM

@@@@@@@@@@@@@@@@@@@@@@@@@@@@@@@

"We've been lucky. So far they've only downsized our cubicles."

A woman in my office recently divorced after years of marriage, had signed up for a refresher CPR course.

"Is it hard to learn?" someone asked.

"Not at all," my coworker replied. "Basically you're asked to breathe life into a dummy. I don't expect to have any problem. I did that for 32 years."

—PAULETTE BROOKS

At the company water cooler, I bragged about my children's world travels: one son was teaching in Bolivia, another was working in southern Italy, and my daughter was completing a yearlong research project in India. One coworker's quip, however, stopped me short. "What is it about you," he asked, "that makes your kids want to get so far away?"

—TODD W. KAISER

Following the announcement of an aggressive cost-cutting program at my company, each employee was encouraged to recommend ways to save money. A couple of days later, I stepped into an elevator where a large poster was hanging to remind workers of an upcoming blood drive. Underneath the huge words "Give Blood," someone had scribbled, "I knew it would come to this."

—CHUCK BRADFORD

The investment management firm where I worked had just moved into new offices, and the place was overflowing with gifts of large plants, mostly huge Boston ferns. Amid this jungle, I was showing off underwater photographs of sea life from a recent scuba-diving trip. Just then a senior member of the firm looked over my shoulder and asked, "Are those anemones?"

"Of course not," I replied. Then, pointing to the plants around us, I quipped, "With ferns like these, who needs anemones?"

—DAVID A. CONARY

Scene: Two coworkers conversing.

Coworker 1: My son just turned 18 months old.
Coworker 2: So, is that like a year and a half old?
Coworker 1: You really aren't sure if 18 months is a year and a half?
Coworker 2: How am I supposed to know that? I don't have kids.

—ADAM FREDERICK

@@@@@@@@@@@@@@@@@@@@@@@@@@@@@@

One day while at work, I called home to talk to my college-student wife, forgetting momentarily that she would be at a class. After leaving a message on our answering machine, I closed with my customary "I love you." As I hung up, I was startled by a coworker who was standing in the doorway and had heard me. With a look of contempt she said, "Your wife is holding on line one."

—JASON LEIFESTER

On my rural postal route, I make deliveries only to roadside mailboxes that are accessible. For two days a woman met me at a disabled tractor that blocked her mailbox. "My husband says he'll move it as soon as he can," she said with a sigh as she accepted the mail.

On the third day the tractor was still there. I expected the woman to appear, but instead saw that the mailbox had been removed from its post. It was now strapped with black tape to the fender of the tractor—at exactly the required height for delivery.

—WILLMA WILLIS GORE

My husband works in a former supermarket that was remodeled to accommodate professional offices. One day he overheard his receptionist giving directions over the phone. "Remember the old grocery store?" she asked the caller. "You'll find us in the meat department."

—KAREN G. STOWE

Following a blowout shindig the night before, a coworker was looking the worse for wear.

"Are you feeling all right?" I asked.

"I don't know," she answered slowly. "I think I'm suffering from post-partying depression."

—MAY-LING GONZALES

Signs you don't have enough to do at work:

- You've already read the entire Dilbert page-a-day calendar for 2012.

- People come to your office only to borrow pencils from your ceiling.

- You discover that staring at your cubicle wall long enough produces images of Elvis.

- The Fourth Division of Paper Clips has overrun the Pushpin Infantry, and General Whiteout has called for reinforcements.

—LYNDELL LEATHERMAN

@@@@@@@@@@@@@@@@@@@@@@@@@@@@@@@

Man to coworker: "I learn more from originals left in the copier than I do from the employee newsletter."

—LITZLER IN *THE WALL STREET JOURNAL*

First thing every single morning one of the secretaries in our office opened the newspaper and read everyone's horoscope aloud.

"Gwen," said our boss finally, "you seem to be a normal, levelheaded person. Do you really believe in astrology?"

"Of course not," Gwen answered. "You know how skeptical we Capricorns are."

—DEAN MORGAN

My daughter is in the cast of a dinner-theater company, which presents mysteries in a local restaurant. While the shows are entertaining, the food leaves a lot to be desired. Near the end of the play, each member of the audience submits a form, answering the question, "Who do you think is the murderer and why?"

"It must be the cook," answered one disgruntled guest. "He tried to poison the rest of us, too."

—A. G. HARTMAN

The brave new memo about the company's revised travel policy read as follows: We were no longer allowed to buy cheap tickets via the Internet. Instead, we were required to use the more expensive company travel department.

Furthermore, to show how much money we were saving, we were asked to comparison-shop for fares—on the Internet.

I thought the typo in the last line of the memo summed it up best: "The new process is ineffective today."

—KIP HARTMAN

QUOTABLE QUOTES

"The Brain is a wonderful organ. It starts working the moment you get up and does not stop until you get into the office."

—ROBERT FROST

"I had the most boring office job in the world—I used to clean the windows on envelopes."

—RITA RUDNER

"How to get a good raise: Request meeting with the boss. Outline accomplishments. Use words such as future and growth. Threaten to quit. Quit. Depart for higher-paying position. You did go in with another job offer, right?"

—TED ALLEN

"A cubicle is just a padded cell without a door."

—UNKNOWN

"A raise is like a martini: it elevates the spirit, but only temporarily."

—DAN SELIGMAN

"The human race is faced with a cruel choice: work or daytime television."

—DAVE BARRY

"You moon the wrong person at an office party and suddenly you're not 'professional' anymore."

—JEFF FOXWORTHY

"It's just a job. Grass grows, birds fly, waves pound the sand. I beat people up."

—MUHAMMAD ALI

"Hard work is damn near as overrated as monogamy."

—HUEY LONG

As a new employee for a discount brokerage firm, I went for a month of classroom training. Warning us about the volume of information we were required to memorize, one instructor suggested we make lots of notes on file cards.

When I completed the course, I was assigned to a team where, as suggested, I taped all the file cards, crammed with notes, onto my computer.

On my first day of trading, a veteran broker sat with me. He immediately noticed all the cards—and my apprehension—and promptly made up a new card, which he taped to my computer. It read "Breathe!"

—STEVE J. GAINES

"Anderson, we'd like to talk to you about your stand-offish attitude."

@@@@@@@@@@@@@@@@@@@@@@@@@@@@@@@@@

Soon after I started a new job, a coworker named Elizabeth showed me how to clear the copier when it became jammed. A few days later the machine jammed again, and I began to punch buttons and slam doors to clear it as I was shown. "What's going on?" asked a colleague.

"I'm clearing the copier like Elizabeth taught me," I replied.

"Oh, but you have to understand," the man explained. "Elizabeth has a temper."

—SHERRY MCNEAL

Even though I've worked in many state government agencies over the years, I still don't get the jargon. Here's an example of what I read every day and—worse—am expected to understand:

"Most of you will be developing subleases instead of subsubleases, so any reference to 'subsubleases' needs to be changed to 'subleases,' except for paragraph 38, which will become 'subsubleases' instead of 'subsubsubleases.' Also, there will no longer be any reference to 'Subsublessor' or 'Subsublessee,' which become 'Sublessor' and 'Sublessee,' respectively. I hope this information will get you started."

—TRUDIE MIXON

The elevator in our building malfunctioned one day, leaving several of us stranded. Seeing a sign that listed two emergency phone numbers, I dialed the first and explained our situation.

After what seemed to be a very long silence, the voice on the other end said, "I don't know what you expect me to do for you; I'm a psychologist."

"A psychologist?" I replied. "Your phone is listed here as an emergency number. Can't you help us?"

"Well," he finally responded in a measured tone. "How do you feel about being stuck in an elevator?"

—CHRISTINE QUINN

I used to work in the business office of a water-slide park where hundreds of high school and college students are employed as lifeguards, gift-shop clerks and food vendors. For many this is a first job. One day I overheard a lunchroom conversation between two teenagers. "So how do you like your job?" one asked.

"I guess it's okay," the other answered, "but it's not at all what I expected."

"What do you mean?" the first teen asked.

"Well, I thought it would be fun working here. I guess I'm more the customer type."

—KARENA SPACH

Extraordinary Excuses

One of my coworkers got a speeding ticket and was attending a defensive-driving course to have points erased from her license. The instructor, a police officer, emphasized that being on time was crucial, and that the classroom doors would be locked when each session began.

Just after one class started, someone knocked on the locked door. The officer opened it and asked, "Why are you late?"

The student replied, "I was trying not to get another ticket." The officer let him in.

—PATTY STEFFER

"Sorry I'm late, boss! I had to take my wife to the maternity ward," Konrád blurts out on arriving at his workplace.

"You don't imagine I'm going to swallow that, do you? That was your excuse last time. Your wife isn't a rabbit after all."

"No, but she's a midwife."

—ZSANETT BAHOR

@@@@@@@@@@@@@@@@@@@@@@@@@@@@@@

"As you both know, here at Frump, Cuttle, and Howsen, failure is not an option. So that only leaves blame."

Dave was late for work. "What's the big idea coming in late?" roared his boss. "The alarm clock woke up everybody but me this morning," said Dave. "What do you mean, it woke up everyone but you?" asked the boss. "You see, there are eight of us in the family, and the clock was set for seven."

— JOVELYN ALCANTARA

@@@@@@@@@@@@@@@@@@@@@@@@@@@@@@@@

Found in a heap of recycled files donated to our school was
this curiously labeled folder: "Excuses I Have Used."

—NANCY EILER

My problem is getting to work on time. One morning,
driving to the office, I came across a turtle in the middle of the
road. I just had to rescue the creature. It took a few minutes for
me to stop the car, grab the turtle and move it off to the side. Then
I rushed on to work.

When I saw my boss at the door, I said quickly, "It's not my
fault, Rich. There was a turtle in the road." Before I could go any
further he bellowed, "So what—you drove behind it?"

—CHRISTY STEINBRUNNER

*15 percent of workers admit to getting to the office late at least once
a week. And here are some of their excuses:*

- "I dreamed I was fired, so I didn't bother to get out of bed."

- "I had to take my cat to the dentist."

- "I went all the way to the office and realized I was still in my
  pajamas and had to go home to change."

- "I saw you weren't in the office, so I went out looking for you."

- "I have transient amnesia and couldn't remember my job."

- "I was indicted for securities fraud this morning."

- "Someone stole all my daffodils."

- "I had to go audition for American Idol."

- "I was trying to get my gun back from the police."

—CAREERBUILDER.COM

@@@@@@@@@@@@@@@@@@@@@@@@@@@@@@@@

While working in the library at a university, I was often shocked by the excuses students would use to get out of paying their fees for overdue books.

One evening an older student returned two books that were way overdue and threw a fit over the "outrageous" $2 fee that I asked her to pay. I tried to explain how much she owed for each day, but she insisted she should be exempt.

"You don't understand," she blurted out. "I didn't even read them!"

—ALISON SATTERFIELD

A friend of mine was running late for work and in her haste to make up time was pulled over for speeding. She pleaded with the police officer, "Please, I don't have much time. I'm already late for work." Pulling out his ticket book, he said soothingly, "Don't worry, Miss. I write very quickly."

—BONA SIJABAT

A big challenge of running a small business is dealing with employees' requests for time off. One morning an employee said, "I need to leave early tomorrow." Later that same day, he followed up with, "Looks like I'll be coming in late tomorrow, but if my coming in late runs into my leaving early, then I won't be in at all."

—JENNIFER KOONTZ

"Why are you late for class every day?" the teacher asks his student. "Because every time I approach the school I see a sign that says **'School. Slow down.'**"

—BLANCA ESTELA ÁLVAREZ

One day a coworker told my husband, Cary, that she was going home early because she didn't feel well. Since Cary was just getting over something himself, he wished her well and said he hoped it wasn't something he had given her. A fellow worker piped up, "I hope not. She has morning sickness."

—BEVERLY WOOD

@@@@@@@@@@@@@@@@@@@@@@@@@@@@@@@

The top things to say when your boss catches you sleeping at your desk:

- "They told me at the blood bank that this might happen."
- "Whew! Guess I left the top off the correction fluid."
- "This is one of the seven habits of highly effective people."
- "Why did you interrupt me? I almost had our biggest problem solved!"
- "Someone must have put decaf in the wrong pot."
- "Ah, the unique and unpredictable circadian rhythms of the workaholic."
- "Amen. Yes, may I help you?"

—SHEILA BRYAN

For the first few months of her co-op position for the state of Georgia, my sister had nothing to do, so she surfed the Web or did crossword puzzles. One day she expressed her boredom to a coworker. "I know," he complained. "Everyone thinks state workers have it easy. But there's only so much you can pretend you're doing."

—MALORY HUNTER

Uncle Jim was late for work when the red lights flashed behind him. Knowing he was busted, Jim pulled over and waited with license and registration in hand.

As the trooper wrote out the ticket, he asked Jim where he was headed.

"I'm late for an important 7:30 meeting," Jim said.

The officer checked his watch.

"If you hurry," he remarked, "you can still make it."

—BILL DAMMAN

When attorney David Loudis was more than two hours late for work, he told his boss this tale of woe: He had awakened thirsty in the middle of the night and, heading for the kitchen, tripped over the cord of his clock radio. The dial began flashing 12:00, indicating that it needed to be reset. After slaking his thirst, he glanced at the kitchen microwave and noted the time—1:06. He returned to his room, reset his clock and fell asleep.

In the morning, the alarm woke him, and he went through his usual routine. Only when he turned on the TV did he discover that the early shows were over and it was 10:30 a.m. In a flash of insight, he realized that the 1:06 had signified not the hour, but the one minute and six seconds of cooking time left after he had prematurely removed some burritos from the microwave the night before.

—LAWRENCE VAN GELDER

Being the office supervisor, I had to have a word with a new employee who never arrived at work on time. I explained that her tardiness was unacceptable and that other employees had noticed that she was walking in late every day.

After listening to my complaints, she agreed that this was a problem and even offered a solution.

"Is there another door I could use?"

—BARBARA DAVIES

One of my jobs as a teacher is checking on the reasons students give for being late or absent. One mother sent a note that explained: **"Please excuse John for being. It was his father's fault."**

—CAROLYN HARRIS

A boss is telling off one of his staff:
"This is the fifth day in a row that you've come late!
What am I supposed to think about that?"

"That today's Friday!"

—WWW.KULICHKI.RU

At a company staff meeting, our president asked a supervisor why his project hadn't been started. The executive sheepishly said that he was waiting for a "go" signal. With that, the president stalked out of the room and returned a few minutes later with the company flag. Standing in front of everyone, he raised the flag and, in race-car fashion, lowered it swiftly while shouting, "Go!"

—RAMON CARLOS J. ABDON

I work in human resources and often meet with employees to discuss workplace problems. During one session, a woman who was having a dispute with one of her colleagues complained that she was "sick and tired of having to argue like a child."

"Well," I offered, "why don't you initiate a meeting with your supervisor and the coworker to discuss your unhappiness?"

"Why should I have to?" she countered. "She started it!"

—ANJELICA T. NATION

My teaching career had led me to an isolated post in the North, where winter temperatures are subzero. One such morning a latecomer handed me a note from her mother, which read: "Sorry Andrea is late. The rooster froze up."

—LEONA KROPF

@@@@@@@@@@@@@@@@@@@@@@@@@@@@@@

A note I received from my student's father: "Please excuse Chris's absence yesterday. Due to my poor planning, my wife had a baby."

—MARY FILICETTI

My wife worked at a country-music radio station in North Carolina where another employee was notorious for the colorful excuses he offered to back up his habitual tardiness. One summer morning when he strolled in late again, the station manager demanded an explanation. "It was so hot today," the straggler said, "that the asphalt molecules in the highway expanded, creating a greater distance between my home and the office."

—PAUL FOERMAN

A vice president of our company was notorious for insisting on punctuality. He fined anyone arriving late for a meeting a dollar. At one gathering, a latecomer asked what the executive did with the money he collected. "It's for my early-retirement fund," he quipped. Immediately, everyone else at the meeting broke out their wallets and added their dollars to the pile.

—CHARLES WOOD

Need a reason for being late to work?

Don't try these—they didn't help any of the workers who actually used them.

- "My deodorant was frozen to the windowsill."
- "My car door fell off."
- "I dreamed I was already at work."
- "I had an early-morning gig as a clown."

—KATE LORENZ

@@@@@@@@@@@@@@@@@@@@@@@@@@@@@@@

Smith goes to see his supervisor in the front office. "Boss," he says, "we're doing some heavy housecleaning at home tomorrow, and my wife needs me to help with the attic and the garage, moving and hauling stuff."

"We're short-handed, Smith," the boss replies. "I can't give you the day off."

"Thanks, boss," says Smith. "I knew I could count on you!"

—JAY TRACHMAN

When one of the salesmen in our office arrived two hours late for work, he sheepishly explained that he and his wife had been arguing the previous night. "If you can't speak to me nicely, you shouldn't speak at all!" he had yelled at her. Then he spent the night on the sofa.

The next morning he awoke to find the sun high, the house quiet and his wife long gone to work. A note on the coffee table beside him said, "Bryan, it's time to wake up."

—JANET FRONKO

Up, Down, and Out

A coworker had a unique scheme to meet women. He'd call numbers at random from the phone book. If a man picked up, he apologized for dialing the "wrong" number.

But when a woman answered, he'd strike up a conversation. One day, the department manager overheard him bragging how he averaged two dates a week from this ploy. Was he fired? Did he receive a reprimand? No, he was named Director of Telemarketing.

—RICHARD REYNOLDS

Anytime companies merge, employees worry about layoffs. When the company I work for was bought, I was no exception. My fears seemed justified when a photo of the newly merged staff appeared on the company's website with the following words underneath:

"Updated daily."

—DIANNE STEVENS

@@@@@@@@@@@@@@@@@@@@@@@@@@@@@@@@

The clinic where I work promoted a coworker to head the payroll department, or Payment Management Systems. The title on his door now reads PMS Director.

—MARILYN PEARSALL

When my boss asked for a computer diskette containing certain data, I took the opportunity to lobby for a raise. The diskette was empty except for the desired information. So, adhering to the eight-character limit, I changed the file name and called it "IncMyPay."

The diskette was returned with a note approving the data, but there was no comment on the file name or the likelihood of a raise. Days later, when I needed to update the file, I noticed the name had again been changed. It was now called "FatChanc."

—LARRY ROACH

Getting fired from my first "real" job wasn't fun, but it was quick. The sports-information director at the University of Kansas summoned me to his office. Without a trace of subtlety, he asked, "Pete, not counting today, how long have you been with us?"

—PETE ENICH

One of my first jobs was with a company that installed swimming pools. My boss called me into his office after a few days to tell me he appreciated my hard work. "As a reward, I'm going to give you a new company vehicle," he said.

At first I was in shock, and then my excitement grew as he talked about the independent front-wheel suspension, air conditioning and the color—cherry red. "This baby will really haul," he said. The next morning my boss drove up and unloaded my new set of wheels—a bright-red wheelbarrow.

—BILLY BABCOCK

@@@@@@@@@@@@@@@@@@@@@@@@@@@@@@@@

Nothing makes your clothes go out of fashion faster than getting a raise.

—*LOS ANGELES TIMES SYNDICATE*

I can't say my friend was heartbroken when her clueless coworker was let go. But she was confused when she saw her at her desk the next day and the day after that.

It all made sense when the "ex" colleague was overheard saying, "So I guess in two weeks, I have to quit."

—JOANNA THOMAS

The boss called an employee into his office. "Bob," he said, "you have been with the company for a year. You started in the mail room, one week later you were promoted to a sales position, and one month after that you were promoted to district manager of the sales department. Just four short months later, you were promoted to vice president. Now it's time for me to retire, and I want to make you the new president and CEO of the corporation. What do you say to that?"

"Thanks," said the employee.

"Thanks?" the boss replied. "Is that all you can say?"

"I guess not," the employee said. "Thanks, Dad."

—RON DENTINGER

Confiding in a coworker, I told her about a problem in our office and my fear that I would lose my job. She was concerned and said she would pray for me. I know she keeps a list of the ten people she believes need her prayers the most, so I asked if she had room for me on her list.

"Oh, yes," she replied. "Three of the people have died."

—KAYE GORDON

Just a few weeks after taking a job as a security guard, my husband announced that he'd been fired.

"What happened?" I asked. He explained that he'd fallen asleep at his desk and someone broke into the building.

"But you're a light sleeper," I said. "I'm surprised the sound of the guy breaking in didn't wake you up."

"I didn't get fired for falling asleep," he confessed. "I was fired for wearing my earplugs."

—ALBERTA J. , FROM CLASSIFIEDGUYS.COM

Shortly after Dad retired, my mother asked him, "What are you going to do today?"

"Nothing," he said.

"That's what you did yesterday."

"Yeah, but I wasn't finished."

—BEVERLY SHERMAN

Retirement is the best thing that has happened to my brother-in-law.

"I never know what day of the week it is," he gloated. "All I know is, the day the big paper comes, I have to dress up and go to church."

—DONALD REICHERT

I've been fired so many times, I sleep in a pink slip.

—TAYLOR NEGRON, *FIRED!* BY ANNABELLE GURWITCH (TOUCHSTONE)

A touching tribute to a waitress, spotted outside a local restaurant: **"RIP Sandy. We will miss you. Server needed."**

—JENNINE MURPHY

ON THE JOB 79

@@@@@@@@@@@@@@@@@@@@@@@@@@@@@@@@

At a company retirement party for Richard, one of my husband's coworkers, the soon-to-be retiree took out a thick stack of notes for his farewell speech. Groans were heard throughout the room, as Richard was known for his verbosity. Moments later, however, Richard was greeted with a standing ovation when he smiled and slowly unfolded the wad of paper into a huge sign that read, "GOOD-BYE, TENSION. HELLO, PENSION."

—LAURA HAWKINS

Steve and Dave were laid off, so they went to the unemployment office. When asked his occupation, Steve replied, "I'm an underwear stitcher. I sew the elastic onto cotton panties."

The clerk looked up "underwear stitcher" and found it classified as unskilled labor. Steve would receive $300 a week in unemployment.

Then it was Dave's turn. When asked his occupation he said, "Diesel fitter." Since diesel fitter was skilled work, Dave would get $600—per week. When Steve found out, he stormed back into the office to complain. The clerk explained that Steve was an unskilled laborer, while Dave was a skilled worker. "Skilled?" said Steve, outraged. "What skill? I sew the elastic on the panties. Then he holds them up and says, 'Yup, diesel fitter.'"

—RICHARD A. WRIGHT

On arriving late to work, an employee was called to the supervisor's office.

"Mr. Morales, you're one of the most valuable employees who have ever worked for this company and, frankly, I don't know what we would do without you."

Timidly, the employee responded: "I'm pleased to hear that you think so highly of me, sir, but why did you call me in?"

"Because tomorrow we are going to find out."

—MARCOS ARAUJO

"Sorry Marcus . . . you've been demoted."

During her retirement party from the Cook County State's Attorney's office, coworkers told stories about my less-than-worldly mother. My favorite came from her supervisor, who recalled one of the first arrest reports Mom had created. Under "Offense," she'd typed, "Possession of cannibals."

—CATHY COTTER

My mother has tried her hand at several careers, some even concurrently. Imagine the surprise of both a hospital patient and my mom when the patient awoke after surgery and, upon seeing who her nurse's aide was, yelled, "What are you doing? You're the woman who helped me pick out interior paint colors!"

—DAN SMITH

Workers usually get the ax for one pretty basic reason: They're not doing the work.

But as the job-search company Simply Hired discovered, reasons for terminating employment are not always that simple.

- I was fired from my job for eating leftover pizza from another department's meeting.

- My partner and I, security guards at a courthouse, were terminated for letting a woman ride on the conveyor belt through the x-ray machine at the front entrance.

- I was fired after I sent company data to someone named Michael Finn. Turns out, I was actually told to send it to "Microfilm."

In honor of my brother's retirement from the police force, my sister-in-law decided to throw a surprise party for him. Plans made in secrecy over a two-month period included catering and entertainment decisions as well as travel accommodations for over 100 friends and relatives from around the country. At the party, my brother stood up to address his guests. As he looked around the room at everyone who had secretly gathered on his behalf, he shook his head and said, "After 25 years on the police force, I finally know why I never made detective."

—LAWRENCE WRIGHT

Our coworker went missing for a few hours, and we tore up the place looking for him. The boss finally found him fast asleep. Rather than wake him, he quietly placed a note on the man's chest. **"As long as you're asleep," it read, "you have a job. But as soon as you wake up, you're fired."**

—KENNETH A. THOMAS

@@@@@@@@@@@@@@@@@@@@@@@@@@@@@@@@

For many years I worked as a receptionist and switchboard operator at a busy company. After a good annual review, my supervisor told me I was up for a raise, pending approval of the vice president.

A month later, my supervisor called me into his office and told me the VP had refused to approve the salary hike. His reason? I clearly wasn't doing my job. Every time he saw me, I was either chatting with someone in the lobby or talking on the telephone.

—J. M. DUTZ

Boss: "I've decided to use humor in the workplace. Experts say humor eases tension, which is important in times when the work force is being trimmed. Knock-knock."

Employee: "Who's there?"

Boss: "Not you anymore."

—SCOTT ADAMS

Hey, things could be worse for you at the office! You could, for example, receive feedback like these comments, purported to be taken from actual federal-employee evaluations:

- "Since my last report, this employee has reached rock bottom and has started to dig."

- "Works well under constant supervision and when cornered like a rat in a trap."

- "Sets low personal standards and consistently fails to achieve them."

- "This employee is depriving a village somewhere of an idiot."

"In other words, we'd like you to start thinking outside of another company's box."

The chairman of the board of our company called me into his office to tell me the good news: I was being promoted to Vice President of Corporate Research and Planning.

Of course I was excited, but that didn't stop me from asking for my new title to be changed to Vice President of Corporate Planning and Research.

"Why?" the chairman asked.

"Because," I said, "our organizational charts list names with abbreviated job titles, and I don't want to be known as Robert E. Reuter, VP of CRAP!"

—ROBERT E. REUTER

For more than an hour a scrawny guy sat at a bar staring into his glass. Suddenly a burly truck driver sat down next to him, grabbed the guy's drink and gulped it down. The poor little fellow burst out crying. "Oh, come on, pal," the trucker said. "I was just joking. Here, I'll buy you another."

"No, that's not it," the man blubbered. "This has been the worst day of my life. I was late for work and got fired. When I left the office I found that my car had been stolen, so I walked six miles home. Then I found my wife with another man, so I grabbed my wallet and came here. And just when I'm about to end it all," the guy said, sobbing, "you show up and drink my poison."

—*PLAYBOY*

The top ten signs your company is planning layoffs:

10. Company softball team downsized to chess team.

9. Dr. Kevorkian hired as a "transition consultant."

8. Pretty young women in marketing suddenly start to flirt with dorky personnel manager.

7. The beer of choice at company picnics is Old Milwaukee.

6. Giant yard sale in front of corporate headquarters.

5. Company president now driving a Hyundai.

4. Annual company holiday bash moved from Sheraton banquet room to abandoned Fotomat booth.

3. Employee discount days at Ammo Attic are discontinued.

2. Company dental plan now consists of pliers and string.

1. CEO frequently heard mumbling "Eeny, meeny, miney, mo" behind closed doors.

—PETER S. LANGSTON

@@@@@@@@@@@@@@@@@@@@@@@@@@@@@@@

I quit my job at the helium gas factory. I refuse to be spoken to in that tone.

—COMIC STEWART FRANCIS

Only a few months before my father's retirement, the insurance company he worked for announced it would relocate to another state. He didn't want to move so late in his career, though, and the company was retaining ownership of the office building, so my father asked if he could stay on in some capacity.

The only available job, they told him, involved watering and caring for the building's many plants. Having little choice, my father trained with a horticulturist for a few weeks and then began his new work.

We worried about how Dad would cope with such a drastic change until he came home one day with new business cards. They read: "Raymond Gustafson, Plant Manager."

—ARLENE MORVAY

There are some predictable phases you go through after you lose a job. I know—I've been through more than half a dozen companies in the last 15 years. Here's what to expect:

- Stage one: I'll make a few phone calls and be working in no time.

- Stage two: None of these jobs in the paper are good enough for me. Now that I've stopped shaving, maybe I'll just stop bathing, too.

- Stage three: Geez, I'm not qualified for any of these jobs, but the house sure is clean.

- Stage four: Maybe I'll try a whole new career. I wonder who's on "Oprah" today? I've got to put something on my unemployment claim this week.

- Stage five: The capitalist running dogs want me to fight for their filthy money? I'm going to weave hats out of palm fronds and sell them on the beach. I won't participate in this sublimation of true human needs.

- Stage six: "You'll pay how much? Well, I've always enjoyed being part of a team!"

—MIKE SPITZ

The Powers That Be

Long, unproductive meetings are often the bane of corporate life. My very funny boss at the software company where I work has come up with what just might be the perfect way to cut business conferences short before they start rambling out of control.

There comes a time when he announces, "All those opposed to my plan say, 'I resign.' " End of meeting.

—BEVIN MATTHEWS

I bought a small sign at a novelty shop that read "I'm the Boss," and taped it to my office door. When I returned from lunch, there was a yellow Post-it note stuck to the sign. "Your wife called," it said. "She wants her sign back."

—KARL ZOLLINGER

On my first day of work at a fishing-supply company, my boss showed me many different types of lures. I asked him if the louder colors actually attracted fish. "I don't know about that," he said, "but they sure do attract the fishermen."

—FRIEDA WOODS

@@@@@@@@@@@@@@@@@@@@@@@@@@@@@@@@

Businessman to colleague, approaching company president's office: "Remember to stay downwind from him. He can smell fear."

—DAVE CARPENTER IN *THE WALL STREET JOURNAL*

I broke my collarbone in a skiing accident, so I was at home when a package arrived. It was a set of golf clubs that I had won from a sales contest at work. Excited, I phoned my boss to tell him about it. "Wonderful!" he said. "We'll have to go out soon and play a few rounds."

I told him I was looking forward to it, but that I wouldn't be able to play for several months because of my injury. "No, no, not with you," said my boss. "I was talking about your new clubs."

—MICHAEL D. PROCTOR

My boss was invited to be the principal speaker at a conference. He was told that he would have plenty of time for his talk, but that he had to finish by the noon lunch break. Unfortunately, the early speakers took longer than scheduled, and he didn't take the lectern until 11:45 a.m. "Well, now I know what principal means," he told the crowd. "It's what's left after the interest is gone."

—SHERRIE H. LILGE

To celebrate his 40th birthday, my boss, who is battling middle-age spread, bought a new convertible sports car. As a finishing touch, he put on a vanity plate with the inscription "18 Again."

The wind was let out of his sails, however, when a salesman entered our office the following week. "Hey," he called out, "who owns the car with the plate 'I ate again'?"

—CINDY GILLIS

Just as our son was learning to walk, my wife brought him to the office. He staggered around awhile, then dropped to his hands and knees and took off at top speed toward the office of the company president. We grabbed him at the doorway, but not before he was noticed by a coworker. "You know," said the employee, turning to my wife, "His father goes into that office the very same way."

—ROBERT N. SORENSEN

@@@@@@@@@@@@@@@@@@@@@@@@@@@@@

Looking for the perfect boss? You won't find one here:

- At work today, I was making a profit-and-loss spreadsheet. "Great, we're in the red!" my boss shouted when he saw it. Then I pointed out that red was bad. "Oh," he said, "I always get those mixed up."

- We were doing icebreakers at a meeting and asked what everybody's favorite Beatles song was. My boss's answer? "Satisfaction." No one corrected him.

- At work today, I spilled a little ketchup on the corner of my suit jacket. My boss then squirted some of his ketchup on the other side so that it would match.

—PHIL EDWARDS AND MATT KRAFT, *DUMBEMPLOYED* (RUNNING PRESS)

"I've got good news and bad news," announced my boss as he came in to work. "The good news: I got the senior discount at the movie theater."

"What's the bad news?" I asked.

"I'm 52."

—PATRIC MCPOLAND

Resolving to surprise her husband, an executive's wife stopped by his office. She found him with his secretary sitting on his lap. Without hesitating, he dictated, "...and in conclusion, gentlemen, shortage or no shortage, I cannot continue to operate this office with just one chair."

—PHIL HARTMAN

Boss to subordinate: "Dan, you're my most valuable employee. Your ineptitude consistently raises the self-esteem of everyone you work with."

—RANDY GLASBERGEN

@@@@@@@@@@@@@@@@@@@@@@@@@@@@@@@@

Boss: "I can assure you that the value of the average employee will continue to increase."

Employee: "That's because there will be fewer of us doing more work, right?"

Boss: "Right. Except for the 'us' part."

—SCOTT ADAMS

I work at a tire store, and one day my boss and I went out to run some errands. While sitting at a traffic light, we saw two young guys in sports cars loudly revving their engines. When the light turned green, they took off with their tires smoking and squealing. "Listen," my boss said, "they're playing our song."

—GARY L. LARSON

I have a reputation at work for being a strict boss. One day I was in the break room with another manager. I reached into the refrigerator for my lunch, which was packed in an Ace Hardware paper bag.

My coworker stopped mid-bite and stared at me, looking a little tense. When I pulled my sandwich out of the bag, he sighed in relief.

"What's the matter?" I asked him.

"Uh, nothing," he replied, "I was beginning to think you really do eat nails for lunch."

—AVIS S. ZABOROWSKI

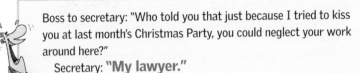

Boss to secretary: "Who told you that just because I tried to kiss you at last month's Christmas Party, you could neglect your work around here?"

Secretary: **"My lawyer."**

—BILL NELSON

@@@@@@@@@@@@@@@@@@@@@@@@@@@@@@@@

My boss mentioned that all our business travel was wearing him down. I said, "Einstein theorizes that as a body approaches the speed of light, it ages at a slower rate. So the more time you spend on jets, the slower you'll age."

"Interesting," my boss said pensively. "But did Einstein take into account airline food?"

—ALEX NEWMAN

I'd had enough of my employees' abusing their allotted break time. In an effort to clarify my position, I posted a sign on the bulletin board: "Starting immediately, your 15-minute breaks are being cut from a half-hour to 20 minutes."

—DON SNYDER

"It's simple, really. You're a team member when *you* want something. You're an employee when *I* want something."

@@@@@@@@@@@@@@@@@@@@@@@@@@@@@@@

To make a long story short, there's nothing like having the boss walk in.

—THE LION

One day my boss showed up for work in a new shirt from her recent trip to Wyoming. It had a picture of trees, a river and the silhouette of a mountain range. "Hey, look," a customer blurted out. "She's got the Grand Tetons on her chest!"

It was the first and last time we saw the shirt.

—DASHA HAGEN

Gail, a neighbor, wanted to buy her workaholic boss a special gift. Knowing that I create handcrafted items as a hobby, she came to me. I made a few suggestions, all of which she said weren't quite right.

Frustrated, Gail asked, "What do I get for a person who has no life?"

"How about a nice urn?" I replied.

—KENNY LEE SKY

A contest was held to find the dumbest things bosses have ever said. The winning—and true!—Dilbert-like entries were:

- "As of tomorrow, employees will only be able to access the building using individual security cards. Pictures will be taken next Wednesday and employees will receive their cards in two weeks."

- "What I need is a list of specific unknown problems we will encounter."

- "This project is so important, we can't let things that are more important interfere with it."

- "Teamwork is a lot of people doing what I say."

The miniature dartboard I received as a gift was housed in a beautiful oak case. I took it to work and showed my friends. Later in the day, my boss came and asked to see it. I proudly showed him the case, but soon discovered our secretaries had a surprise for me: they'd placed a photo of the boss right on the bull's-eye.

—RANDY WEECE

A boss is telling off an employee who has arrived late:

"It's not enough that you don't do your job properly, but you even allow yourself to be two hours late. If I were you, I wouldn't have bothered coming to work at all."

"That's you," retorts the employee, "but I have a sense of duty."

—PAVEL KRUGLOV

Finally, after years of testing business software, I landed my dream job—trying out computer games. My first day at work I was listing various ideas in a spreadsheet program when my manager walked by.

He looked at my screen for a moment, then said sternly, "I'd better not catch you using spreadsheets on company time when you know you should be playing games."

—JON BACH

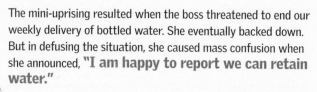

The mini-uprising resulted when the boss threatened to end our weekly delivery of bottled water. She eventually backed down. But in defusing the situation, she caused mass confusion when she announced, **"I am happy to report we can retain water."**

—ROBINETTE FLYGARE

"QUOTABLE QUOTES

"No man goes before his time/unless the boss leaves early."

—GROUCHO MARX

"If you think your teacher is tough, wait until you get a boss. He doesn't have tenure."

—BILL GATES

"If you think your boss is stupid remember; you wouldn't have a job if he was smarter."

—ALBERT GRANT

"Do not underestimate your abilities. That is your boss's job."

—UNKNOWN

"I always try to go the extra mile at work, but my boss always finds me and brings me back."

—ANONYMOUS

"A boss creates fear, a leader confidence. A boss fixes blame, a leader corrects mistakes. A boss knows all, a leader asks questions. A boss makes work drudgery, a leader makes it interesting."

—RUSSELL H. EWING

"Accomplishing the impossible means only that the boss will add it to your regular duties."

—DOUG LARSON

"I don't want any yes-men around me. I want everyone to tell me the truth— even if it costs him his job."

—SAMUEL GOLDWYN

"It's for the boss. He's having a really bad day."

My wife, June, answers her boss's phone as part of her duties. One day his wife dialed his cell phone by accident. "Why didn't June pick up for you?" she asked her husband. "Be glad she didn't," June heard her boss reply. "You just dialed the phone I wear on my belt."

—DOUG MURRAY

@@@@@@@@@@@@@@@@@@@@@@@@@@@@@@@

Supervisor to employee: "Don't think of me as the boss. Think of me as a coworker who's always right."

—*NEWSPAPER ENTERPRISE ASSOCIATION*

No matter how bad the situation, nothing at our school gets in the way of a day off. Case in point, this e-mail I received from our boss: "We will be out of the office Thursday and Friday," it stated. "Please hold all emergencies until Monday."

—CHRISSY CLARKE

Husband to wife: "Well, no, I didn't get the raise...but the boss pointed out a tax loophole I didn't know about!"

—DICK TURNER

As an executive vice president, my father was scheduled to meet with the board of directors of the large advertising agency where he worked. It was Thanksgiving eve, and he and my mother had exchanged numerous telephone calls all day to arrange for the arrival of family members from far away. Their plan finally set, Dad made his way to the meeting. Meanwhile, Mom had come up with a better plan. She called my dad at work, and insisted that his secretary deliver the message to him immediately. The secretary entered the boardroom and announced, "Excuse me, Mr. Harbert, but your wife just called with an urgent message. She said to tell you that she's figured out a new way to do it."

—RICHARD N. HARBERT

Did you hear about the Pepsi exec who got fired?
He tested positive for Coke.

PHILLIP REGULINSKI

When my boss returned to the office, he was told that everyone had been looking for him. That set him off on a speech about how indispensable he was to the company.

"Actually," interrupted his assistant, "you left with the key to the stationery closet."

—ALEC KAY

When my printer's type began to grow faint, I called a local repair shop where a friendly man informed me that the printer probably needed only to be cleaned. Because the store charged $50 for such cleanings, he told me, I might be better off reading the printer's manual and trying the job myself.

Pleasantly surprised by his candor, I asked, "Does your boss know that you discourage business?"

"Actually it's my boss's idea," the employee replied sheepishly. "We usually make more money on repairs if we let people try to fix things themselves first."

—MICHELLE R. ST. JAMES

Many employers motivate workers with bonuses. Some offer gym memberships. A few even supply day care for their working mothers and fathers. Our bosses go a step further. A sign posted in our break room read: "New Incentive Plan...Work or Get Fired!"

—SUSAN RHEA

My boss's tantrum climaxed with him falling out of his chair and hitting the floor. I rushed to his office, but was halted by his secretary. "If he's hurt," she said, "he'll call me in. If he isn't, he won't forgive you for finding him on the floor, and you'll be fired. If he's dead, what's your hurry?"

—BECQUET.COM

"We'll take a short break in case anyone needs to change their underwear."

@@@@@@@@@@@@@@@@@@@@@@@@@@@@@@@

Management always needs to have the last word. Case in point: During a meeting at our financial consulting firm, a coworker was asked to guesstimate a realistic closing rate for the larger cases we were handling. "I'd have to say 20 percent," he answered. "No, no, no," interrupted my boss. "It's more like one in five."

—DAVID ARMSTRONG

"Do you believe in life after death?" the boss asked one of his younger employees.

"Yes, sir."

"Well, then, that makes everything just fine," the boss went on. "about an hour after you left yesterday to go to your grandfather's funeral, he stopped in to see you."

—DOROTHEA KENT

Expert
Antics

"Find a joy you like and you add five days to every week."

—H. JACKSON BROWN, JR.

@@@@@@@@@@@@@@@@@@@@@@@@@@@@@@@@

Law and Order

I am a prosecuting attorney in a small Mississippi town and will admit to having a few extra pounds on me. Not long ago, I was questioning a witness in an armed robbery case. I asked, "Would you describe the person you saw?"

The witness replied, "He was kind of short and stout."

"You mean short and stout like me?" I asked.

"Oh, no," the witness said. "He wasn't that fat."

—WILLIAM E. GOODWIN

When I worked in the law library of the South Carolina attorney general's office, one of my duties was to handle subscriptions to various law journals. I usually printed the material carefully because I had a habit of crossing double t's so close to each other that they resembled an H.

On a particularly busy day, however, I filled out a subscription renewal form too quickly and mailed it in. A few weeks later, as I was sorting the mail, I came across the renewed publication, now addressed to "A Horney General's Office."

—RHONDA H. MCCRAY

I'm a police officer and occasionally park my cruiser in residential areas to watch for speeders. One Sunday morning I was staked out in a driveway, when I saw a large dog trot up to my car. He stopped and sat just out of arm's reach. No matter how much I tried to coax him to come for a pat on the head, he refused to budge.

After a while I decided to move to another location. I pulled out of the driveway, looked back and learned the reason for the dog's stubbornness. He quickly picked up the newspaper I had been parked on and dutifully ran back to his master.

—JEFF WALL

"But boss, when you said to apply for a *bailout,*
I thought you meant for the company."

@@@@@@@@@@@@@@@@@@@@@@@@@@@@@@@

Two lawyers walked into the office one Monday
morning talking about their weekends. "I got a dog
for my kids this weekend," said one.

The other attorney replied,
"Good trade."

—CHARLES M. NELMS

Our four-month-old son accompanied my wife and me to our
attorney's office to sign some papers because we couldn't get a
sitter. Unfortunately, it took longer to transact our business than
we planned, and eventually the baby was screaming at the top of
his lungs.

"Maybe we should close the door," my wife suggested, "so this
noise won't bother your colleagues."

"Don't worry," our lawyer said. "They'll just think another
client has received our bill."

—NARAYAN KULKARNI

My uncle testified at the trial of an organized-crime boss
and then begged to be put into the witness-protection program.
Instead, the FBI got him a job as a salesclerk at Kmart. It's been six
months and no one's been able to find him.

—JAY TRACHMAN

I was eager to perform well in my new job as a receptionist
at a law firm. One day a lawyer asked me to type up a letter
that would be sent to the creditors of a man who had recently
passed away. I was mortified, therefore, when soon after turning
in the letter, I heard howling laughter from my boss's office. The
beginning of the letter read, "To all known predators."

—JOANNA B. PARSONS

@@@@@@@@@@@@@@@@@@@@@@@@@@@@@@@

I was in juvenile court, prosecuting a teen suspected of burglary, when the judge asked everyone to stand and state his or her name and role for the court reporter.

"Leah Rauch, deputy prosecutor," I said.

"Linda Jones, probation officer."

"Sam Clark, public defender."

"John," said the teen who was on trial. "I'm the one who stole the truck."

—LEAH RAUCH

In my job as a legal secretary, I often review documents that list the allegations and responses from the defendant such as "admitted," "denied" or "have no knowledge or information to answer." One day my boss received a response from a defendant who apparently did not have the benefit of counsel. His written reply to the allegations? "Did not!"

—SHARON A. PETERSON

After making numerous calls to 911, a Lundar, Canada, man was warned that the next one would land him in jail. That prompted him to give his real reason for calling: "If you're coming to get me," he told the dispatcher, "can you bring me some smokes.

—*WINNIPEG FREE PRESS*

My son, a West Virginia state trooper, stopped a woman for going 15 miles over the speed limit. After he handed her a ticket, she asked him, "Don't you give out warnings?"

"Yes, ma'am," he replied. "They're all up and down the road. They say, **'Speed Limit 55.'**"

—PATRICIA GREENLEE

"My car has been tipped over and rammed repeatedly. You don't know anything about this do you, Carl?"

I'm a deputy sheriff and was parked near a motel, running radar checks, when a man approached my vehicle and asked for help. He complained that the volume on the television in the empty motel room next to his was so loud that he and his wife couldn't sleep. No one was in the motel office.

The man's wife was outside when I reached their door. That's when I got my idea. I asked her for their remote control, aimed it through the window of the empty room, and turned off the blaring TV.

—RAY ALLEN

@@@@@@@@@@@@@@@@@@@@@@@@@@@@@@@@@

I was working the graveyard shift as a rookie police officer one night when my partner and I made a routine check at a high school that had suffered a recent rash of vandalism. Right away I noticed a window was open, so we climbed in to investigate.

We tried to be quiet as we made our way across the room in the dark, but our feet were sticking to the floor and making a squishy noise with every step. Finally when we got to the doorway, I flicked on the light. Looking back, I could easily make out our footprints on the freshly painted concrete floor. The window was open for ventilation, not vandalism.

—JEFFREY A. MOORE

As a state trooper, I drive a motor home to various weigh stations. It serves as our office on wheels while we conduct truck inspections. When the motor home is in reverse, it makes a repetitive beeping noise. One quiet morning I backed the unit out of its carport and stopped alongside my regular patrol car to retrieve something. As I walked toward the car, I heard the familiar beeping sound. My heart stopped as I turned, expecting to see the $80,000 vehicle backing itself down the driveway.

To my relief, the motor home was not moving. But at the top of a nearby tree sat a mockingbird perfectly mimicking the beep.

—JON LINDLEY

I glanced out my office window and saw that police had surrounded the motel across the road. A SWAT team had been dispatched, and people in the restaurant next door were being evacuated.

We soon learned that two armed suspects were holed up in the motel. I phoned my husband at work and described the unfolding drama. When I finished, my husband asked, "Did you call for anything special or just to chat?"

—VIVIAN J. HARTER

@@@@@@@@@@@@@@@@@@@@@@@@@@@@@@@@

During an anti-harassment seminar at work, I asked, "What's the difference between harassment and good-natured teasing?" A coworker shouted, **"A million dollars."**

—MARK STEPHENSON

I picked up the phone one day in the law office where I worked, and the caller asked to speak with an attorney. I didn't recognize the voice, so I asked his name. He gave it to me, saying our office had just served him with divorce papers.

I couldn't place his name right away because this was a new case. Eager to talk, he blurted out, "I'm the despondent!"

—CAROLINE NIED

The mine operator called the nearby state prison and asked them to send over a safecracker to open his jammed safe. Soon, a convict and a prison guard showed up at the office. The inmate spun the dials, listened intently and calmly opened the safe door. "What do you figure I owe you?" asked the mine operator.

"Well," said the prisoner, "the last time I opened a safe, I got $25,000."

The sheriff's office in Alamance County, North Carolina, tried everything to stop people from using fake IDs to get a driver's license, but to no avail. Fed up, wrote the News & Record (Greensboro, North Carolina), one industrious sheriff's deputy concocted an ingenious plan, never before tried. He marched into the DMV waiting room and asked that everyone "with false IDs please step forward."

Six did.

—KATH YOUNG

@@@@@@@@@@@@@@@@@@@@@@@@@@@@@@@@

I answered a 911 call at our emergency dispatch center from a woman who said her water broke.

"Stay calm," I advised. "Now, how far apart are your contractions?"

"No contractions," she said breathlessly. "But my basement is flooding fast."

—PAT HINTZ

When I stopped by his office, our company's security chief was laboring over a memo he was writing announcing a class about the proper use of cayenne pepper spray for personal self-defense.

"I need a good title," he said. "Something catchy that will get people's attention so they'll want to come."

I pondered for a moment and then said, "How about 'Assault and Pepper'?"

—BOB McFADDEN

My mother is on staff at the Department of Motor Vehicles, and one day a close friend of hers came in to apply for a driver's license. While entering the information into a computer, my mom noticed the woman had given 150 pounds as her weight.

Knowing she weighed considerably more, my mom commented, "You're putting down your weight as 150?"

"If a policeman pulls me over," her friend said with a grin, "that's the part of me he'll see."

—GINA BREMMER

When a Middletown, New Jersey, police officer retired, he cited low morale. But he didn't leave quietly. While walking the beat on his last day, he wrote 14 tickets for expired inspection stickers...all to police patrol cars.

—ASSOCIATED PRESS

@@@@@@@@@@@@@@@@@@@@@@@@@@@@@@@@

Early in my career as a judge, I conducted hearings for those involuntarily committed to our state psychiatric hospital. On my first day, I asked a man at the door of the hospital, "Can you tell me where the courtroom is?"

"Why?" he asked.

"I'm the judge."

Pointing to the building, he whispered, "Don't tell them that. They'll never let you out."

—CHRISTOPHER DIETZ

My wife was raised in Sweden, yet speaks English without an accent. She does, however, sometimes confuse her idioms.

One day a man entered the law office where she works as a secretary. Using a Swedish phrase, but not quite translating it right, she asked, "May I help you take your clothes off?"

Startled by her remark, the man stepped back. Realizing what she had said and trying to put him at ease, she added, "It's okay, really. I'm Swedish."

—ROBERT E. ALEXANDER

When I worked for the security department of a large retail store, my duties included responding to fire and burglar alarms. A side door of the building was wired with a security alarm, because it was not supposed to be used by customers. Nevertheless they found the convenience of the exit tempting. Even a sign with large red letters warning "Alarm will sound if opened," failed to keep people from using it.

One day, after attending to a number of shrieking alarms, I placed a small handmade sign on the door that totally eliminated the problem: "Wet Paint."

—L. J. HINES-JOHNSON

@@@@@@@@@@@@@@@@@@@@@@@@@@@@@@@

The woman in front of me at the motor vehicles office was taking the eye test, first with her glasses on, then off. "Here's your license," the examiner said when she was done. "But there's a restriction. You need to wear glasses to drive your car."

"Honey," the woman declared, "I need them to find my car."

—NICOLE HAAKE

"Fine print doesn't work anymore—the reader can just change the font size."

@@@@@@@@@@@@@@@@@@@@@@@@@@@@@@@@

Executive behind desk to prospective employee: **"It's always cozy in here. We're insulated by layers of bureaucracy."**

—COTHAM IN *THE NEW YORKER*

Chris was sent to prison, and the warden made arrangements for him to learn a trade. In no time, Chris became known as one of the best carpenters in the area, and often got passes to do woodworking jobs for people in town.

When the warden started remodeling his kitchen, he called Chris into his office and asked him to build and install the cabinets and countertops. Chris refused.

"Gosh, I'd really like to help you," he said, "but counterfitting is what got me into prison in the first place."

An investment banker decides she needs in-house counsel, so she interviews a young lawyer.

"Mr. Peterson," she says. "Would you say you're honest?"

"Honest?" replies Peterson. "Let me tell you something about honesty. My father lent me $85,000 for my education, and I paid back every penny the minute I tried my first case."

"Impressive. And what sort of case was that?"

"Dad sued me for the money."

—DEE HUDSON

While working as a corrections officer at a maximum-security prison, I was assigned to the guest area one day to monitor the inmates and their visitors.

I received a call from the reception desk, and was told there was a cab out front, probably waiting for one of the visitors.

Sticking my head into the room, I announced, "Did anyone call for a cab?"

About 40 inmates immediately raised their hands.

—JANET E. HUMPHREY

@@@@@@@@@@@@@@@@@@@@@@@@@@@@@@@

The fist knocking on the door belonged to a cop. Bracing for the worst, my husband, who was working on a job site, opened up.

"Is that yours?" asked the officer, pointing to a company van that was jutting out into the narrow street.

"Uhh, yes, it is," said my husband.

"Would you mind moving it?" asked the officer. "We've set up a speed trap and the van's causing everyone to slow down."

—JUNE STILL

I am a deputy sheriff assigned to courthouse security. As part of my job, I explain court procedures to visitors. One day I was showing a group of ninth graders around. Court was in recess and only the clerk and a young man in custody wearing handcuffs were in the courtroom.

"This is where the judge sits," I began, pointing to the bench. "The lawyers sit at these tables. The court clerk sits over there. The court recorder, or stenographer, sits over here. Near the judge is the witness stand and over there is where the jury sits.

"As you can see," I finished, "there are a lot of people involved in making this system work."

At that point, the prisoner raised his cuffed hands and said, "Yeah, but I'm the one who makes it all happen."

—MICHAEL MCPHERSON

Our community still has teenage curfew laws. One night I was listening to my scanner when the police dispatcher said, "We have a report of a 14-year-old male out after curfew. The subject, wearing jeans and a gray sweatshirt, is six-foot-four and weighs 265 pounds." After a long pause, one of the patrols replied, **"As far as I'm concerned, he can go anywhere he wants."**

—JAMES VAN HORN

@@@@@@@@@@@@@@@@@@@@@@@@@@@@@@

Hired by a bank as a personal trainer, I was supposed to make fitness a part of the workday routine. During one session, I told my students to lean against the bank lobby's walls and instructed them on how to stretch their hamstrings. A short time later I was shocked when several policemen stormed through the doors. A passerby had seen the people facing the wall and assumed I was robbing the bank.

—SYLVIA DOUGHART-WOOD

What's Up, Doc?

I was working as an interpreter at a hospital when I found myself in the middle of an odd conversation. The doctor warned his patient, "By drinking and smoking as much as you do, you're killing yourself slowly."

The patient just nodded. "That's OK. I'm not in any hurry."

—SALMA SAMMAKIA,

As I performed a simple medical procedure on my patient, I warned her, "After this, you can't have sex for at least three days."

"Did you hear that?" she asked her husband. "No sex for three days."

"I heard," he said. "But she was speaking to you."

—KATHLEEN HOWELL

When my daughter was home during college break, she came in for an eye exam at the optometrist's office that I manage. I gave her some paperwork to fill out, and had to laugh when I read what she had written under method of payment: **"My mom."**

—SHIRLEY KUDRNA

@@@@@@@@@@@@@@@@@@@@@@@@@@@@@@@@

A man walked into our medical practice complaining that he was in agony.

"Where exactly is the pain?" asked his doctor.

"Near my ovaries," he moaned.

"You don't have ovaries."

The patient looked confused. "When were they removed?"

—KELLI EAST

My nursing colleague was preparing an intravenous line for a 15-year-old male patient. The bedside phone rang, and the boy's mother reached over to pick it up.

After talking for a few minutes, the mother held the phone aside, turned to her son and said, "Your dad is asking if you've got any cute nurses."

The boy gazed at the nurse, who had the needle poised above his arm, ready for insertion.

"Tell him," he replied, "they're absolutely gorgeous."

—MATTHEW HUTCHINSON

My mother and I were at the hospital awaiting some test results when several firemen were wheeled into the emergency room on stretchers. One young man was placed in the cubicle next to us. A hospital employee began to ask him questions so she could fill out the necessary paper work. When he was asked his phone number, we had to laugh. His reply? "911."

—VICTORIA VELASCO

My 60-year-old mother-in-law, completing two years of wearing orthodontic braces, was in the office having them adjusted. As she sat in one of the waiting-room chairs, the teenager next to her looked at my mother-in-law in astonishment.

"Wow," he said. "How long have you been coming here?"

—DAVID REEVES

"Don't you hate it when there are parts left over?"

As a doctor I receive calls at all hours of the day. One night a man phoned and said, "I'm sorry to bother you so late, Doc, but I think my wife has appendicitis."

Still half asleep I reminded him that I had taken his wife's inflamed appendix out a couple of years before. "Whoever heard of a second appendix?" I asked.

"You may not have heard of a second appendix, Doc, but surely you've heard of a second wife," he replied.

—JAMES KARURI MUCHIRI

@@@@@@@@@@@@@@@@@@@@@@@@@@@@@@@

I'm an obstetrics nurse at a large city hospital, where our patients are from many different countries and cultures.

One day while waiting for a new mother to be transferred to our division, I checked the chart and assumed that, because of her last name, she was of European descent. So when she was finally wheeled in, I was surprised to see that she was Asian.

As I was performing the exam, we chatted and she told me she was Chinese and her husband's ethnic heritage was Czech. After a short pause she quipped, "I guess that makes my children Chinese Czechers!"

—LISA M. EDGEHOUSE

While I sat in the reception area of my doctor's office, a woman rolled an elderly man in a wheelchair into the room. As she went to the receptionist's desk, the man sat there, alone and silent.

Just as I was thinking I should make small talk with him, a little boy slipped off his mother's lap and walked over to the wheelchair. Placing his hand on the man's, he said, "I know how you feel. My mom makes me ride in the stroller, too."

—STEVE ANDERSON

I hate the idea of going under the knife. So I was very upset when the doctor told me I needed a tonsillectomy. Later, the nurse and I were filling out an admission form. I tried to respond to the questions, but I was so nervous I couldn't speak.

The nurse put down the form, took my hands in hers, and said, "Don't worry. This medical problem can easily be fixed, and it's not a dangerous procedure."

"You're right. I'm being silly," I said, feeling relieved. "Please continue."

"Good. Now," the nurse went on, "do you have a living will?"

—EDWARD LEE GRIFFIN

@@@@@@@@@@@@@@@@@@@@@@@@@@@@@@@

Overheard outside my medical office—one woman complaining to another: **"My doctor says I have masculine degeneration and that I'll just have to live with it."**

—NANCY K. KNIGHT

My dentist's office was in the midst of renovation when I arrived for a checkup. As the hygienist led me to a room, I could hear the sound of hammering and sawing coming from next door. "It must really scare your patients to hear that when they're in the dentist's chair," I remarked.

"That's nothing," she said. "You should see what happens when they hear the jackhammer."

—CHUCK ROTHMAN

At the outpatient surgery center where I worked, the anesthesiologist often chatted with patients before their operations to help them relax. One day he thought he recognized a woman as a coworker at the VA hospital where he had trained. When the patient confirmed that his hunch was correct, he said, "So, tell me, is the food still as bad there as it used to be?"

"Well," she replied, "I'm still cooking it."

—SHEILA HOWARD

A man walks into a cardiologist's office.
Man: "Excuse me. Can you help me? I think I'm a moth."
Doctor: "You don't need a cardiologist. You need a psychiatrist."
Man: "Yes, I know."
Doctor: "So why'd you come in here if you need a psychiatrist?"
Man: "Well, the light was on."

—HEATHER BORSDOR

@@@@@@@@@@@@@@@@@@@@@@@@@@@@@@@@@

On the job as a dental receptionist, I answered the phone and noticed on the caller-ID screen that the incoming call was from an auto-repair shop.

The man on the line begged to see the dentist because of a painful tooth.

"Which side of your mouth hurts?" I asked the patient.

He sighed and answered, "The passenger side."

—CHERYL PACE SATTERWHITE

I was working with a doctor as he explained to his patient and her concerned husband what would happen during and after her upcoming surgery. Then the doctor asked if there were any questions.

"I have one," said the husband. "How long before she can resume housework?"

—JONATHAN JACOB

My father is a successful cardiologist, but his busy practice and long hours left my mother with a lot of spare time. So she decided to become a substitute teacher.

At the end of her first month on the job, she bought my father a new watch. "Honey, I just spent my whole month's salary on a gift for you," she said. "It's now your turn to do the same."

—RAHUL TONGIA

The husband of one of our obstetrics patients phoned the doctor to ask if it would be okay to make love to his wife while he was taking medication for an infected foot.

"Yes, that's fine," the doctor replied. **"Just don't use your foot."**

—SABRINA HENDERSON

@@@@@@@@@@@@@@@@@@@@@@@@@@@@@@

While visiting my mother in the hospital, I stopped in the cafeteria for breakfast. I set a piece of bread on the moving toaster rack and waited for it to pass under the heated coils and return golden brown. Instead, it got stuck at the back of the toaster and I couldn't reach it. The woman next in line quickly seized a pair of tongs, reached in and fished out the piece of toast. "You must be an emergency worker," I joked.

"No," she replied with a grin. **"I'm an obstetrician."**

—BECKY LEIDNER

My husband, a doctor, received an emergency call from a patient: She had a fly in her ear. He suggested an old folk remedy. "Pour warm olive oil in your ear and lie down for a couple of minutes," he said. "When you lift your head, the fly should emerge with the liquid."

The patient thought that sounded like a good idea. But she had one question: "Which ear should I put the oil in?"

—BELINDA HIBBERT

A harried man runs into his physician's office. "Doctor! Doctor! My wife's in labor! But she keeps screaming, 'Shouldn't, couldn't, wouldn't, can't!'"

"Oh, that's okay," says the doctor. "She's just having contractions."

—DONNA WINSTON

Just because one owns a business doesn't mean it has to be all business. This sign in a dentist's office proves that point: "Be True to Your Teeth, or They Will Be False to You."

—JAMES WERTZ

@@@@@@@@@@@@@@@@@@@@@@@@@@@@@@@

The doctor is called late at night to a woman in labor. He goes into the room and closes the door. After a while he calls out. "Could I have some pliers, a screwdriver, and a hammer, please."

Turning deadly pale, the husband cries out, "For God's sake, what are you doing?"

"Take it easy, I'm only trying to open my bag."

—BOGNÁR JÁRFÁS

The patient who came to my radiology office for abdominal X-rays was already heavily sedated. But I still had to ask her a lot of questions, the last one being, "Ma'am, where is your pain right now?"

Through her medicated fog, she answered, "He's at work."

—JEFF DOTY

In our pediatric office, I answered the phone to hear a frantic parent say she was at a Chinese restaurant, and her son had gotten a piece of paper lodged in his nostril.

They came over, and the doctor examined the boy. When the exam-room door opened, the doctor was holding the fortune from the child's cookie. It read "You will prosper in medical research."

—KERRI PACE JACKSON

Exasperated with obnoxious patients in the clinic where she's the office manager, my aunt put up a sign that read: "If you are grouchy, irritable, or just plain mean, there will be a $10 surcharge for putting up with you."

Clearly some people took the sign to heart. That same afternoon a patient came to her window and announced, "The doctor said he would like to see me every month for the next six months, so I'm going to pay all my $60 up front."

—JUSTINE A. BACARISAS

@@@@@@@@@@@@@@@@@@@@@@@@@@@@@@@@

The doctor's office was crowded as usual, but the doctor was moving at his usual snail's pace. After waiting two hours, an old man slowly stood up and started walking toward the door.

"Where are you going?" the receptionist called out.

"Well," he said, "I figured I'd go home and die a natural death."

—SIMON BJERKE

Paying my bill at the doctor's office, I noticed one of the clerks licking and sealing a large stack of envelopes. Two coworkers were trying to persuade her to use a damp sponge instead. One woman explained that she could get a paper cut. Another suggested that the glue might make her sick. Still, the clerk insisted on doing it her own way.

As I was leaving, I mentioned to the clerk that there was a tenth of a calorie in the glue of one envelope. Then I saw her frantically rummaging around for the sponge.

—DOROTHY MCDANIEL

One afternoon a very preoccupied looking young woman got on my bus. About 15 minutes into the ride, she blurted out, "Oh, my gosh, I think I'm on the wrong bus line."

I dropped her at the next stop and gave her directions to the right bus. "I don't know where my mind is today. I must have left it at work," she apologized.

Just before she got off, I noticed she was wearing an ID card from an area hospital. "Are you a nurse?" I asked.

"Oh, no," she said. "I'm a brain surgeon."

—RACHELLE ROCK

@@@@@@@@@@@@@@@@@@@@@@@@@@@@@@@@

Even though it was warm outside, the heat was on full blast in my office at the hospital. So I asked our nursing unit secretary to get someone to fix it. This was a one-man job, so I could not figure out why two guys showed up—until I was handed the maintenance request form. It read: "Head nurse is hot."

—CAROLYN HOUSE

While taking a patient's medical history, I asked if anyone in her family had ever had cancer.

"Yes," she said. "My grandmother."

"Where did she have it?"

"In Kansas."

—DIXIE LEGGETT

Our crew at an ambulance company works 24-hour shifts. The sleeping quarters consist of a large room with several single beds, so we get to know one another's habits, like who snores or talks in their sleep.

While I was having my teeth examined by a dentist one day, he noticed that some of my teeth were chipped. "It looks like you clench your jaw at night," he said.

"No way," I blurted without thinking. "No one has ever said I grind my teeth, and I sleep with a lot of people!"

—KELLY WILSON

A man walks into a psychiatrist's office.

"Doc, every time I see nickels, dimes, and quarters, I have a panic attack! What can my problem be?"

"Oh, that's easy," the doctor answers. **"You're just afraid of change."**

—WAYNE BENNETT

@@@@@@@@@@@@@@@@@@@@@@@@@@@@@@@

Time is a great healer. **That's why they make you wait so long in the doctor's office.**

—RON DENTINGER

Last Valentine's Day, I arrived at the doctor's office where I work as a receptionist to find a mystery man pacing up and down holding a package. As I got out of the car, he declared warmly, "I have something for you." I excitedly ripped open the bundle. It was a urine sample.

—HEATHER BOYD

Every so often I'd challenge a father visiting his newborn in the nursery, where I was a nurse, to guess his baby's weight. Few even came close, but one dad picked up his son, hefted him in his hands, and gave me the precise weight, right down to the ounces.

"That was amazing," I told him.

"Not really," he replied. "I do this all the time. I'm a butcher."

—NOLA FARIA

It was a busy day in the doctor's office where I worked, and I was on the phone trying to arrange a patient's appointment. Needing her daytime phone number, I hurriedly asked, "May I have a number between eight and five, please?"

After a moment came the timid response, "Six?"

—DEBORAH SIMONS

We were helping customers when the store optometrist walked by and smiled at a coworker. Of course, we all had to stop what we were doing to tease her. But she quickly dismissed the notion of a budding romance. "Can you imagine making out with an optometrist?" she asked. "It would always be, 'Better like this, or like this?'"

—JESS WEDLOCK

@@@@@@@@@@@@@@@@@@@@@@@@@@@@@@@

Nothing seemed out of the ordinary when a patient's file arrived at our clerk's office in the hospital—nothing, that is, until I read the doctor's orders. He had written, "Chest pain every shift, with assistance if necessary."

—PARR YOUNG

When a patient was wheeled into our emergency room, I was the nurse on duty. "On a scale of zero to ten," I asked her, "with zero representing no pain and ten representing excruciating pain, what would you say your pain level is now?"

She shook her head. "Oh, I don't know. I'm not good with math."

—DON ANDREWS, RN

While I was on duty at a Los Angeles-area hospital as a registered nurse, a man arrived in an ambulance, accompanied by his wife and a neighbor. "I'm worried about my husband," I overheard the wife say to her friend. "Since we just moved here, I know nothing about this hospital."

"Don't worry," her neighbor replied. "The doctors and nurses here are excellent. I should know—this is where my husband died."

—MARGARET A. FRICE

Jack was depressed when he got back from the doctor's office. "What's the matter?" his wife asked.

"The doctor says I have to take one of these white pills every day for the rest of my life."

"And what's so bad about that?"

"He only gave me seven."

—*ROTARY DOWN UNDER*

@@@@@@@@@@@@@@@@@@@@@@@@@@@@@@@@@@

My ten-year-old son Andrew and I were waiting in a dentist's office, talking about treatments for his painful tooth. Entering the room, the dentist asked, "Well, Andrew, which one's the troublemaker?" Without hesitation Andrew replied, "My brother."

—BELINDA SMITH

One day after a heavy snowfall, this announcement appeared on the bulletin board in the nurse's lounge of my local hospital: "Student nurses will please refrain from ever again using this institution's sterile bedpans for makeshift snow sleds."

—JILL MARIE BONNIER

Employed as a dental receptionist, I was on duty when an extremely nervous patient came for root-canal surgery. He was brought into the examining room and made comfortable in the reclining dental chair. The dentist then injected a numbing agent around the patient's tooth, and left the room for a few minutes while the medication took hold.

When the dentist returned, the patient was standing next to a tray of dental equipment.

"What are you doing by the surgical instruments?" asked the surprised dentist.

Focused on his task, the patient replied, "I'm taking out the ones I don't like."

—DR. PAULA FONTAINE

One day while at the doctor's office, the receptionist called me to the desk to update my personal file. Before I had a chance to tell her that all the information she had was still correct, she asked, **"Has your birth date changed?"**

—MARGARET FREESE

@@@@@@@@@@@@@@@@@@@@@@@@@@@@@@@

Seen on a car parked outside a gynecologist's office: **PUUUSH.**

—CAROLE GROMADZKI

After practicing law for several months, I was talking with my brother, John, a doctor. "My work is so exciting," I said. "People come into my office, tell me their problems and pay me for my advice."

As older brother will, John took the upper hand. "You know," he said, "in my work, people come into my office, tell me their problems, take off all their clothes and then pay me for my advice."

—DAVID PAUL REUWER

While working as a radiologic technologist in a hospital emergency room, I took X-rays of a trauma patient. I brought the films to our radiologist, who studied the multiple fractures of the femurs and pelvis.

"What happened to this patient?" he asked in astonishment.

"He fell out of a tree," I reported.

The radiologist wanted to know what the patient was doing up a tree. "I'm not sure, but his paperwork states he works for Asplundh Tree Experts."

Gazing intently at the X-rays, the radiologist blinked and said, "Cross out 'Experts.'"

—GENIEVE MARKOVCI

It took me forever to wake up one of my nursing home patients. But after much poking, prodding, and wrangling, he finally sat up and fixed his twinkling blue eyes on my face. "

My, you're pretty!" he said. "Have I asked you to marry me yet?"

"No, you haven't," I gushed.

"Good. Because I couldn't put up with this every morning."

—DIANE WITLOX

Airport Hijinks

"What's the difference between an optimist and a pessimist?" I asked my husband. He thought for a minute before responding, "An optimist is the guy who created the airplane. A pessimist is the guy who created the parachute."

—SUZAN WIENER

@@@@@@@@@@@@@@@@@@@@@@@@@@@@@@@@

On a late Sunday night flight from Sydney to Brisbane, most passengers looked tired, harassed, and desperate to get off the plane. So did the cabin crew. As we were taxiing to the terminal, the steward started his spiel about remaining in your seats until the plane came to a standstill. He ended with, "Thank you for flying with us and be careful when opening the overhead toilets, which may have moved during the flight."

—GLENDA FORKNALL

After setting off the alarms at airport security, I was escorted behind a curtain. As two female officials "wanded" me, the senior officer gave instructions to the trainee on proper technique: first down the front of my body, then up the back of me, and—much to my embarrassment—up between my legs.

After she was done, her boss congratulated her. "Great job," she said. "Now do it again. But this time, try turning on the wand."

—VICTORIA RADFORD

A helicopter loses power over a remote Scottish island and makes an emergency landing. Luckily, there's a cottage nearby, so the pilot knocks on the door. "Is there a mechanic in the area?" he asks the woman who answers.

She thinks for a minute. "No, but we do have a McArdle and a McKay."

En route to Hawaii, I noticed one of my passengers in the coach section of the airplane dialing her cell phone. "Excuse me. That can't be on during the flight," I reminded her. "Besides, we're over the ocean—you won't get a signal out here."

"That's okay," she said. "I'm just calling my daughter. She's sitting up in first class."

—DAWN CALLAHAN

@@@@@@@@@@@@@@@@@@@@@@@@@@@@@@@

I wouldn't want to fly Virgin. **Who'd want to fly an airline that doesn't go all the way?**

—ADAM J. SMARGON

As an airline reservation agent, I took a call from a man who wanted to book a flight for two but wasn't happy with the price of $59 per ticket. "I want the $49 fare I saw advertised," he insisted, saying he would accept a flight at any time.

I managed to find two seats on a 6 a.m. flight. "I'll take it," he said, then worried that his wife might not like the early hour.

I warned there was a $25 fee per person if he changed the reservation. "Oh, that's no problem," he said dismissively. "What's fifty bucks?"

—ANNA ZOGG

When I worked in airline reservations, we had an executive desk, which did bookings for corporate clients during the day. One evening the phone rang and rang. Finally our supervisor picked it up and said in a monotone, "We are open from 8 a.m. to 5 p.m. Please call back then."

A voice on the other end asked, "Is this a recording?"

Without thinking, my boss replied, "Yes, it is."

—ANNETTE MURRAY

As a flight attendant for a commuter airline, I constantly struggle to keep people seated until the aircraft has come to a complete stop at the gate. So one day, after making the standard announcement, I added, "Those of you who would like to stay and assist me in cleaning up the cabin, please volunteer by standing up before the seat-belt sign is turned off." No one moved—and my solution has worked ever since.

—MARIE WHITEIS

@@@@@@@@@@@@@@@@@@@@@@@@@@@@@@@@

Working as a secretary at an international airport, my sister had an office adjacent to the room where security temporarily holds suspects.

One day, security officers were questioning a man when they were suddenly called away on another emergency. To the horror of my sister and her colleagues, the man was left alone in the unlocked room. After a few minutes, the door opened and he began to walk out. Summoning up her courage, one of the secretaries barked, "Get back in there, and don't you come out until you're told!"

The man scuttled back inside and slammed the door. When the security people returned, the women reported what had happened.

Without a word, an officer walked into the room and released one very frightened telephone repairman.

—RUSS PERMAN

Plane Ridiculous

With airlines adding fees to fees, The Week *magazine asked its readers to predict the next surcharge they'll levy for something previously free.*

- In the unlikely event of loss of cabin pressure, oxygen masks will drop down. To start the flow of oxygen, simply insert your credit card.

- $100 On-Time Departure Fee; $25 Delay-Complaint Fee

- View seating (formerly window seats), $10; Access seating (formerly aisle seats), $10

- $20 to use roll-away stairs to enter or exit the aircraft in lieu of no-charge rope-ladder alternative

- $9 fee for bumping your head on the overhead bin as you take your seat; $3 additional penalty for looking up at the bin after you bump into it

@@@@@@@@@@@@@@@@@@@@@@@@@@@@@@@@

The flight attendant will always tell you the name of your pilot. **Like anyone goes, "Oh, he's good. I like his work."**

—DAVID SPADE

I'm a captain with a major airline, and I routinely monitor the flight attendants' announcements while taxiing to the gate. Impatient passengers often stand up and attempt to dash forward before we arrive. Once, instead of the usual terse voice reminding people to remain in their seats, I heard the attendant declare, "In the history of our airline, no passenger has ever beaten the aircraft to the gate. So, ladies and gentlemen, please remain seated."

—JOE CONFORTI

My father's colleague was on a company plane when, immediately after takeoff, a wheel fell off. The pilot did not want to land with a full fuel tank, so he circled through some heavy turbulence. When he finally touched down, he managed to tilt the plane, balancing it on only two tires until it had almost stopped.

As the pilot came out of the cabin to see if everyone was all right, the passengers noticed his name tag. It read "Bond."

—ILA COLTAS

During a business trip to Boeing's Everett, Wash., factory, I noticed several 747 and 777 airliners being assembled.

Before the engines were installed, huge weights were hung from the wings to keep the planes balanced. The solid-steel weights were bright yellow and marked "14,000 lbs."

But what I found particularly interesting was some stenciling I discovered on the side of each weight. Imprinted there was the warning: "Remove before flight."

—KEVIN N. HAW

@@@@@@@@@@@@@@@@@@@@@@@@@@@@@@@

My wife, a flight attendant for a major airline, watched one day as a passenger overloaded with bags tried to stuff his belongings in the overhead bin of the plane. Finally, she informed him that he would have to check the oversized luggage.

"When I fly other airlines," he said irritably, "I don't have this problem."

My wife smiled and replied, "When you fly other airlines, I don't have this problem either."

—JOE CONFORTI

Sales and Service Slip-ups

I took a part-time job as an opinion-poll sampler, calling people for their views on various issues. On my very first call, I introduced myself, "Hello, this is a telephone poll." The man replied, "Yeah, and this is a street light!"

—ANDY GOLAN

Working for a florist, I took a call from a woman who spoke to me over a very crackly cell phone. She wanted to send a wreath to a friend's funeral, but I couldn't make out what message she wanted to accompany the flowers. Finally, I just had to interrupt her. "It's a bad line," I said over the din. There was a slight pause before she said, "Well, can you think of something better to say?"

—IVOR EDWARDS

A customer who bought a book from me through amazon.com left a poor rating. The reason: "The book was dated."

The title of the book was Victorian Fancy Stitchery.

—MOIRA ALLEN

@@@@@@@@@@@@@@@@@@@@@@@@@@@@@@@@

Even though telemarketers are slightly less beloved than dentists and tax auditors, that's the job my friend took during his summer vacation. Halfway through one of his sales pitches, he heard a clicking at the other end of the line. Thinking the man may have hung up, he asked, "Are you still there?"

"Yeah, still here," said the man.

"Sorry, I heard a click and I thought you'd been disconnected."

"No," the man said, "that would sound more like this." He then proceeded to show me what it would sound like by slamming down the phone.

—TRAVIS JAMES

My wife, a real estate agent, wrote an ad for a house she was listing. The house had a second-floor suite that could be accessed using a lift chair that slid along the staircase. Quickly describing this feature, she inadvertently made it sound even more attractive: "Mother-in-law suite comes with an electric chair."

—MICHAEL KIMMIT

Two salesmen, Joe and Mike, were stranded by a winter storm and took refuge in an old farmhouse occupied by an attractive single woman. In the middle of the night, Joe heard Mike sneak out of bed and into the woman's room. Joe said nothing about it until nine months later when a registered letter arrived at his office. Clutching the letter, he walked into Mike's office. "Do you remember the night we were stranded by that snowstorm and you sneaked out of your room to be with that woman?" he asked.

"Yes," Mike replied.

"You told her you were me, didn't you?" Joe demanded.

"Yes, I did," Mike said nervously. "Why do you ask?"

"Because," Joe replied, "she just died and left me a fortune!"

—ALICE L. SMITH

@@@@@@@@@@@@@@@@@@@@@@@@@@@@@@@@@

My daughter and her husband were with us on vacation in Las Vegas, staying in a posh new hotel. As we were lounging by the pool, my son-in-law, whose company builds homes in the Phoenix area, used his cell phone to try to reach his salesmen.

After several unsuccessful attempts, he called his office. "Tell me something," we heard him say. "Am I the only one working today?"

—PAUL JENNINGS

@@@@@@@@@@@@@@@@@@@@@@@@@@@@@@@@@

Dearth of a Salesman

Corporate America lives and dies on the back of its sales force.
Based on the following stories, some companies are DOA:

- "We had a salesman who visited monthly and told me stories of his drunken escapades. After six months, I told him I was a Mormon and didn't care for them. He apologized and then joked, 'So how many wives you got?'"

- "A salesman spelled my name wrong in his presentation. It's Smith."

- "The all-male ad-agency team told my female marketing team that they understood tampons better than us."

—JIM NICHOLS

Trying to sell ads for my high school yearbook, I approached my father, who owned a house painting business with my two brothers. My father agreed to purchase an ad and said I should ask my brother Jack to write it.

"We're too busy now!" Jack protested. "If we run an ad, we'll just get more work."

"Jack," I replied, "Dad said you have to write the ad."

The next morning, Jack handed me his copy. It read, "John J. Pitlyk & Sons, Painting Contractors. For easy work, call the sons. If it's hard, call Pop."

—JOAN PITLYK

The restaurant we had lunch in is one business that knows how to handle dissatisfied customers. On the wall was an open bear trap and this sign: **"To Register Complaint, Push Button."**

—MARK VELEZ

@@@@@@@@@@@@@@@@@@@@@@@@@@@@@@@@@

Seen in a John Deere sales office: **"The only machine we don't stand behind is our manure spreader."**

—NORMAN HAUGLID

A sales representative stops at a small manufacturing plant in the Midwest. He presents a box of cigars to the manager as a gift. "No, thanks," says the plant manager. "I tried smoking a cigar once and I didn't like it."

The sales rep shows his display case and then, hoping to clinch a sale, offers to take the manager out for martinis. "No, thanks," the plant manager replies. "I tried alcohol once, but didn't like it."

Then the salesman glances out the office window and sees a golf course. "I suppose you play golf," says the salesman. "I'd like to invite you to be a guest at my club."

"No, thanks," the manager says. "I played golf once, but I didn't like it." Just then a young man enters the office. "Let me introduce my son, Bill," says the plant manager.

"Let me guess," the salesman replies. "An only child?"

My father is a skilled CPA who is not great at self-promotion. So when an advertising salesman offered to put my father's business placard in the shopping carts of a supermarket, my dad jumped at the chance. Fully a year went by before we got a call that could be traced to those placards.

"Richard Larson, CPA?" the caller asked.

"That's right," my father answered. "May I help you?"

"Yes," the voice said. "One of your shopping carts is in my yard and I want you to come and get it."

—MATTHEW LARSON

@@@@@@@@@@@@@@@@@@@@@@@@@@@@@@@

Tech Talk

The company I work for boasts a high-tech check-in system that enables our staff to monitor who is, and isn't, in the office. Recently I asked a secretary if a particular supervisor was in. She agreed to find out, and left the room. When she returned a few moments later, I asked her if she had been using the new system to see if he was clocked in.

"No," she replied. "I was looking out the window to see if his car is here."

—BILL WILLIAMS

Now that my mother's office has a fax machine, I fax my correspondence to her instead of using the post office. Although I've told her many times that it's a faster and less expensive way to communicate, she continued to mail me weekly letters.

On my last birthday, however, she showed that she now has a full grasp of technology. She faxed me a $100 bill with the note: "Happy Birthday. You're right—it is cheaper to fax than mail. Love, Mom."

—SUSAN REILLY

In the office where I work, there is a constant battle between our technical-support director and customer-service personnel over the room temperature, which is usually too low.

The frustrated director, trying to get us to understand his position, announced one afternoon, "We need to keep the temperature below seventy-five degrees or the computers will overheat."

Thinking that this was just another excuse, one of my shivering colleagues retorted, "Yeah, right. So how did they keep the computers from overheating before there was air conditioning?"

—HEIDI DYSARD

@@@@@@@@@@@@@@@@@@@@@@@@@@@@@@@

"It's not personal, Carlyle. I just downloaded a new phone app that will replace you."

During a lecture on the influence of media on teens, a typo in the PowerPoint presentation revealed the professor's true opinion. The title read: "Three Reasons Teens Are Vulnerable Toads."

—MICHAEL DOBLER

@@@@@@@@@@@@@@@@@@@@@@@@@@@@@@@@

After a lengthy course on improving computer skills, a teacher finally seemed to get the hang of it. In fact, he admitted in his self-evaluation, **"Computers have simplified and shortened my life."**

—BART ALTENBERND

One night, a few coworkers at the computer data center where I work stayed late, and we all started to get hungry. We decided to order in food by phone, but our boss thought that, since we work with computers, it would be more appropriate to order by Internet. After we contacted the fast food chain's Web site and spent a long time registering as new customers for the delivery service, a message appeared on the screen: "Thank you for your business. You will be able to order food in three days."

—THANTHIP RIOTHAMMARAT

Before retiring from my 30-year marketing career at IBM, I attended a seminar where a young salesman presented the latest PC. Impressed with the presentation, I remarked, "When I joined the company, we intended to make the computer as easy to use as the telephone. It looks like we made it."

"We have," the speaker replied. "We've made the phone a lot more complicated."

—LYNN A. SMITH

The new computer system at work allowed us to e-mail messages to one another. Soon after it was installed, my boss saw me at lunch and asked me for some reports, adding, "I left a message on your computer."

I had to laugh when I got back to my desk. There I saw his message—taped to the computer screen.

—JEANNE WASHBURN

@@@@@@@@@@@@@@@@@@@@@@@@@@@@@@@@@@

A technology fanatic, my boss is adamant about creating a paperless office. Away on a business trip, he had left instructions on my voice mail: "Fax the contract revisions to your PC, then forward the fax to my e-mail box. When the transmission is complete, send a message to my digital-display pager. Then I will call you from my cellular phone with further instructions."

Just after I finished listening to his message, though, my boss called back. He had forgotten his modem and now wanted me to send the documents to him by overnight mail.

—RENEE EAREGOOD

Learning new computer skills can be a challenge. An office manager in my software training class, taking nothing for granted, jotted down every word.

During a recent session, I peeked over his shoulder and read what he'd written: "New Computer Training—password is first name...Mine is Bob."

—TIMOTHY FOUBERT

"HTML code is automatically generated by Fireworks when you export, copy, or update HTML," stated our highly technical computer manual. But in case technophobes should begin to panic, it went on to explain, "You do not need to understand it to use it."

—KATE LINDON

During a break at the plant where I'm employed, I walked by a friend who works with computers. He was sitting at his desk with his feet propped up, staring straight ahead as if in a trance. When he didn't stir as I passed, I asked, "Are you all right?"

He blinked, smiled and said, **"I'm on screensaver."**

—ALBERT F. BECKER

@@@@@@@@@@@@@@@@@@@@@@@@@@@@@@@

My husband and I are both in an Internet business, but he's the one who truly lives, eats, and breathes computers.

I finally realized how bad it had gotten when I was scratching his back one day.

"No, not there," he directed. **"Scroll down."**

—CHRISTINE AYMAN

The computer in my high school classroom recently started acting up. After watching me struggle with it, one of my students took over. "Your hard drive crashed," he said.

I called the computer services office and explained, "My computer is down. The hard drive crashed."

"We can't just send people down on your say-so. How do you know that's the problem?"

"A student told me," I answered.

"We'll send someone over right away."

—ROLF EKLUND

I was looking over some computer hardware at an electronics store when I overheard a customer tell the salesclerk, "I'd like a mouse pad, please."

"We have loads to choose from, sir," answered the clerk.

"Great," said the customer. "Will they all be compatible with my computer?"

—SNEHAL SHAH

"Pardon me," said the young man. I looked up from behind my desk at the library. "How do I get on the computer?"

"Just tell us your name and wait," I answered.

"Okay, it's John," he said, "125 pounds."

—LORI RICHARDSON

@@@@@@@@@@@@@@@@@@@@@@@@@@@@@@@

At the radio station where I worked, the manager called me into his office to preview a new sound-effects package we were considering purchasing. He closed the door so we wouldn't bother people in the outer office. After listening to a few routine sound effects, we started playing around with low moans, maniacal screams, hysterical laughter, pleading, and gunshots. When I finally opened the door and passed the manager's secretary, she looked up and inquired, "Asking for a raise again?"

—NANCY ERVIN

In an attempt to complete its fiscal year figures on time, our company's finance department one day posted this sign outside its offices: "Year-end in progress. Please be quiet."

Our network specialist, whose office is right next door, put up this notice in response: "Shhh...quiet please. Information Technology works all year."

—LINDA MCGRAW

As a new federal employee, I felt a combination of excitement and anxiety about meeting the strict standards of discretion and respect that our government imposes on its workers. Fearful of making a costly mistake, I decided to read up on procedures and standards on the federal Office of Personnel Management web page. I'm not sure if I was relieved or worried when I clicked on one page and found: "Ethics: Coming Soon!"

—JAMES RESTIVO

After being on the phone forever with a customer who had been having difficulties with a computer program, a support technician at my mother's company turned in his report: "The problem resides between the keyboard and the chair."

—NICOLE MILLIGAN

"I don't understand it, sir, the computers have only been down for an hour."

I had always considered myself a with-it communicator of the '90s. But I had no clue what my friend was saying recently when he pointed out a "Double Beamer."

"What do you mean by 'Double Beamer'?" I asked.

With a grin he replied, "An IBM employee driving a BMW."

—KAY L. CAMPBELL

@@@@@@@@@@@@@@@@@@@@@@@@@@@@@@@

My husband, Brian, is a computer systems administrator. He is dedicated to his job and works long hours, rarely taking time off for meals.

One afternoon, Brian was overwhelmed with solving a computer network problem, so I decided to deliver a meal for him to eat at his workstation.

When I was getting ready to leave, I said good-bye and reminded him to eat his burger and fries while they were still warm.

Staring at his monitor, he waved me away. "Don't worry," he said, obviously distracted, "I'll delete them in a few minutes."

—MICHELLE HILL

Manning the computer help desk for the local school district was my first job. And though I was just an intern, I took the job very seriously. But not every caller took me seriously.

"Can I talk to a real person?" a caller asked.

"I am real," I said.

"Oh, I'm sorry," the caller said. "That was rude of me. What I meant to say was, could I talk to someone who actually knows something?"

—SHARRON JONES

As I was cleaning my computer keyboard with a can of air duster (compressed chemicals), I noticed a slew of warnings: "Do not breathe fumes!" "Use only in well-ventilated areas!" "Avoid contact with skin and eyes!" And in BIG, impossible-to-miss letters: "INTENTIONAL MISUSE BY DELIBERATELY INHALING CONTENTS CAN BE FATAL!"

Then, I turned over the can. There, I found a symbol with a tree in it. Surrounding it were the words "Environmentally Friendly."

—SHARON BACON

My techie husband and I were walking in the high desert when he stopped to photograph one stunning vista after another. Overcome by the sheer beauty, he paid it his ultimate compliment:

"Everywhere I look is a screen saver!"

—LAURIE EYNON

My husband, Jeff, and I incurred several problems while assembling our new computer system, so we called the help desk. The man on the phone started to talk to Jeff in computer jargon, which confused us even more. "Sir," my husband politely said, "please explain what I should do as if I were a four-year-old."

"Okay," the computer technician replied. "Son, could you please put your mommy on the phone?"

—LENA WORTH

Driving on the interstate, I saw a vehicle with the license: ALT F7. I checked my computer at home, and as I suspected it was a Word-Perfect command. The truck had to belong to a plumber. Who else would choose the command: "Flush Right"?

—RUTHANN NICHOLS

Over the years I have heard my share of strange questions and silly comments from people who call the computer software company where I work as a tech support telephone operator. But one day I realized how absurd things can sound on the other end of the line when I heard myself say to one caller, "Yes, sir, you must first upgrade your download software in order to download our upgrade software."

—CARLOS MEJIA

@@@@@@@@@@@@@@@@@@@@@@@@@@@@@@@@

On my way to deliver a computer to a customer, I saw a handwritten sign at the entrance of an alley. It read: "Blocked! Do not pass! Difficult to turn back." I continued anyway, only to discover that the alley was indeed blocked by a fallen tree.

As predicted, it took a while to turn the truck around. When I finally got back to the entrance, I noticed a second sign. It read: "Told you so!"

—IRWAN WIJAYA

I couldn't have been happier the day I figured out how to play my favorite CDs on my computer at the office while simultaneously doing my work. One day I was enjoying Beethoven when an administrative assistant delivered a stack of papers. Hearing classical music fill the air, she shook her head and said, "Don't you hate it when they put you on hold?"

—BENNY J. WURZ

No doubt about it, the new temp hadn't a clue about computers. Since part of her job was directing calls to our technical support department, I gave her simple instructions: "When people call with computer problems, always ask which operating system they're using—Windows, Macintosh or UNIX."

Later, she handed a technician this phone message. "Call immediately," she'd written. "Customer has problem with eunuchs.

—SUSAN CROFT

Powering up his office computer one morning, my colleague saw a unique error message: "Keyboard undetected."

Then he saw how he was supposed to clear the error: **"Press any key to continue."**

—DAVID BAUER

@@@@@@@@@@@@@@@@@@@@@@@@@@@@@@@@

A computer company had a seemingly impossible problem with a very expensive machine. Staff engineers tried everything they could think of, but they couldn't fix it. Desperate, they contacted a retired engineer with a reputation for repairing all things technical. The engineer spent a day studying the huge machine. With a piece of chalk he marked the trouble spot with an X. The part was replaced, and the machine worked perfectly again. But when the company's accountants received the engineer's bill for $50,000, they demanded an itemized tally of his charges.

The engineer responded: One chalk mark, $1. Knowing where to put it, $49,999.

A coworker asked if I knew what to do about a computer problem that was preventing her from getting e-mail. After calling the help desk, I told my colleague that e-mail was being delayed to check for a computer virus.

"It's a variant of the I Love You virus, only worse," I said.

"What could be worse?" my single coworker asked wryly. "The Let's Just Be Friends virus?"

—ARTHUR J. ORCHEL

With five kids at home and one more on the way, I wasn't quite sure what to think when I was assigned the following password for my computer at work: "iud4u."

—CAROLYN THOMAS

I work in a busy office where a computer going down causes quite an inconvenience. Recently one of our computers not only crashed, it made a noise that sounded like a heart monitor. "This computer has flat-lined," a coworker called out with mock horror. **"Does anyone here know how to do mouse-to-mouse?"**

—MARY BOSS

@@@@@@@@@@@@@@@@@@@@@@@@@@@@@@

The latest term being bandied about our IT office is PICNIC: "Problem In Chair, Not In Computer."

—ARLIN JOHNSON

The chef of the upscale restaurant I manage collided with a waiter one day and spilled coffee all over our computer. The liquid poured into the processing unit, and resulted in some dramatic crackling and popping sounds.

After sopping up the mess, we gathered around the terminal as the computer was turned back on.

"Please let it work," pleaded the guilt-ridden waiter.

A waitress replied, "Should be faster than ever. That was a double espresso."

—BRIAN A. KOHLER

I was a computer-savvy student, so the high school librarian called me to her office complaining of a computer crash. While booting up the computer, I asked her what she had done immediately prior to the crash. "I just erased some files that were taking up memory space," she replied matter-of-factly. "There was one big one that the Spanish teacher, Señorita Dobias, must have put on there. I think it was called DOS."

—BRANDIE LITTLETON

At work, my dad noticed that the name of an employee was the same as that of an old friend. So he found the man's e-mail address and sent him a message. When Dad received a reply, he was insulted. So he fired back another e-mail: "I have put on some weight, but I didn't realize it was that noticeable!"

His friend's hastily typed message, with an apparent typo, had read, "Hi, Ron. I didn't know you worked here, but I did see a gut that looked like you in the cafeteria."

—BRAD CARBIENER

Divine Duties

The pastor of my church hates to plead for money. But when the coffers were running low, he had no choice. "There's good news and there's bad news," he told the congregation "The good news is that we have more than enough money for all the current and future needs of the parish. The bad news is, it's still in your pockets."

—GILES V. SCHMITT

"What's the difference between a Catholic priest and a minister?" our daughter Sarah asked.

My husband, a pastor, answered, "Well, one big difference is that a priest can't marry. That's because he's expected to devote his life to God. A pastor also dedicates his life to God, but he can marry. It's like having your cake and eating it too."

Sarah's next question: "Priests can't eat cake?"

—JO-ANNE TWINEM

During our priest's sermon, a large plant fell over right behind the pulpit, crashing to the ground. Acknowledging his reputation for long-windedness, he smiled sheepishly and said, "Well, that's the first time I actually put a plant to sleep."

—DAVID BERGER

A Catholic priest I once knew went to the hospital to visit patients. Stopping at the nurses' station, he carefully looked over the patient roster and jotted down the room number of everyone who had "Cath" written boldly next to his name.

That, he told me, was a big mistake. When I asked why, he replied, "It was only after I had made the rounds that I learned they were all patients with catheters."

—DENNIS SMYTH

@@@@@@@@@@@@@@@@@@@@@@@@@@@@@@@@

> **"But wasn't God the Father, Son, and Holy Spirit the ultimate multi-Tasker?"**

As church treasurer, he had two computer files labeled "St. Mary's Income" and "St. Mary's Expenditure." While copying them from a Macintosh to a PC, he had no idea the PC would automatically truncate the file names to ten characters, eliminate spaces and replace apostrophes with periods.

Now the church's income is stored in "StMary.sin" and expenses in "StMary.sex."

—CHRISTINE THIEN

@@@@@@@@@@@@@@@@@@@@@@@@@@@@@@@

One Sunday, while serving as a guest minister to a local church, I noticed in the program an order of worship with which I was unfamiliar. Since the service had already begun, I was unable to ask anybody about it. So when we reached that particular moment, I swallowed my pride and asked from the pulpit, "What do I do now?"

Someone in the congregation shouted back, "You say something and we respond."

Embarrassed, I admitted, "For the first time in my life, I'm speechless."

And the congregation responded, "Thanks be to God."

—BEN POWELL

While I was preaching in a church in Mississippi, the pastor announced that their prison quartet would be singing the following evening. I wasn't aware there was a prison in the vicinity and I looked forward to hearing them. The next evening, I was puzzled when four members of the church approached the stage. Then the pastor introduced them. "This is our prison quartet," he said, "behind a few bars and always looking for the key."

—RAYMOND McALISTER

My appointment as pastor coincided with the church's appeal for aid for victims of a hurricane.

Unfortunately, on my first Sunday in the parish, the center page of the church bulletin was accidentally omitted. So members of the congregation read from the bottom of the second page to the top of the last page: "Welcome to the Rev. Andrew Jensen and his family...the worst disaster to hit the area in this century. The full extent of the tragedy is not yet known."

—ANDREW JENSEN

@@@@@@@@@@@@@@@@@@@@@@@@@@@@@@@@@

When our minister and his wife visited our neighbor,
her four-year-old daughter answered the door.
"Mom!" she yelled toward the living room.
"God's here, and he brought his girlfriend."

—KRISTEN KIMBALL

When a nun collapsed in the sales representative's office at
our time-share resort, the rep ran to the front-desk manager.

"Two nuns walked into the sales office, and one of them
fainted!" she yelled breathlessly.

Unfazed, the manager just looked at her.

"Well," said the rep, "aren't you going to do anything?"

He replied, "I'm waiting for the punch line."

—DONNA CAPLAN

Having grown up just outside New York City, I barely knew
a cow from an ear of corn. Until, that is, I married a small-town
Ohio girl. While I was in seminary school, I had a temporary
assignment at a church in a rural community. The day of my first
sermon, I tried very hard to fit in. Maybe too hard. With my wife
sitting in the first pew, I began my discourse: "I never saw a cow
until I met my wife."

—THE REV. LOUIS LISI, JR.

My friend opened a ministry, using a snippet from the Bible
as the name. But he soon regretted his decision to order office
supplies over the phone. When his stationery arrived, it bore the
letterhead: "That Nun Should Perish."

—TOM HARRISON

@@@@@@@@@@@@@@@@@@@@@@@@@@@@@@@@

That's Academic

When I was 28, I was teaching English to high school freshmen in a school where occasionally the faculty and staff were allowed to dress down.

One of those days I donned a sweatshirt and slacks. A student came in and his eyes widened.

"Wow!" he exclaimed. "You should wear clothes like that every day. You look twenty, maybe even thirty years younger!"

—MARY NICHOLS

At a cross-curricular workshop for teachers, several of us from the English department found ourselves assigned to a math presentation. In the middle of the lesson, I leaned over to a colleague and whispered, "Are you getting any of this?"

He shook his head. "Math and I broke up in the '80s, and now it's really awkward whenever we get together."

—BECKY POPE

At a planning meeting at my college, I congratulated a colleague on producing some superb student-guidance notes explaining how to combat plagiarism.

"How long did it take you to write them?" I asked.

"Not long," he said. "I copied them from another university's website."

—BOB WHEELER

While I was an office worker at the local high school, a student stopped by to turn in a lost purse. I gave it to the principal so he could look inside for some type of identification. Moments later his concerned voice could be heard over the intercom: "Liz Claiborne, please come to the office. We have found your purse."

—KATY HYCHE

@@@@@@@@@@@@@@@@@@@@@@@@@@@@@@@@

When my niece's coworker, Eula, began a job as an elementary-school counselor, she was eager to help. One day during recess she noticed a girl standing by herself on one side of a playing field while the rest of the kids enjoyed a game of soccer at the other. Eula approached and asked if she was all right. The girl said she was.

A little while later, however, Eula noticed the girl was in the same spot, still by herself. Approaching again, Eula offered, "Would you like me to be your friend?"

The girl hesitated, then said, "Okay." Feeling she was making progress, Eula then asked, "Why are you standing here all alone?"

"Because," the little girl said with great exasperation, "I'm the goalie."

—BOBBYE J. DAVIS

One of my students could not take my college seminar final exam because of a funeral. No problem, I told him. Make it up the following week. That week came, and again he couldn't take the test due to another funeral.

"You'll have to take the test early next week," I insisted. "I can't keep postponing it."

"I'll take the test next week if no one dies," he told me.

By now I was suspicious. "How can you have so many people you know pass away in three weeks?"

"I don't know any of these people," he said. "I'm the only gravedigger in town."

—SRINIVAS NIPPANI

Discovered: why our nation's education system is in trouble. When a friend delivered 20 new math books to a teacher's classroom, the teacher exclaimed, "Oh, shoot! I was hoping it was something I could use."

—ANGELA TIMPSON

@@@@@@@@@@@@@@@@@@@@@@@@@@@@@@@

"You need to be careful when writing comments," our principal told the faculty. He held a report card for a Susan Crabbe. A colleague had written, **"Susan is beginning to come out of her shell."**

—MARGARET WHARF

A linguistics professor was lecturing his class. "In English," he explained, "a double negative forms a positive. In some languages, such as Russian, a double negative is still a negative.

"However," the professor continued, "there is no language in which a double positive can form a negative."

A voice from the back of the room piped up, "Yeah, right."

—E. T. THOMPSON

When our students began raising donations for Child Abuse Prevention Week, the school administration did its part by setting up a collection box outside the principal's office and displaying a banner by the front door of the lobby. It read "Please give $1 to help stop child abuse in the front office."

—ANGELA LONG

After lunch at a restaurant with five other teachers, my friend Shirley realized they'd forgotten to ask for separate checks. To figure out how much each owed, the tab was passed around the table. The group laughed and chattered through the whole ordeal.

When they finally rose to leave, the man in the next booth grinned at Shirley. "You ladies sure are having a great time," he remarked. "What business are you in?"

"All teachers," she said proudly.

"Ah," he replied. "I knew you weren't accountants."

—WILLMA WILLIS GORE

@@@@@@@@@@@@@@@@@@@@@@@@@@@@@@@@

During the college speech course I taught, I spoke about a Chinese student who, after moving to the United States, decided she wanted an English name to honor her new home.

"She chose the name Patience," I told the class, "because she wanted to be reminded to be patient. Every time someone called her name, the message was reinforced."

I asked the students what names they would select for themselves. After considering the question, one young man raised his hand and said, "Rich."

—JOAN WALDEN

"Ms. Henson, you're going in for Ms. Simms."

@@@@@@@@@@@@@@@@@@@@@@@@@@@@@@

As a band instructor at an elementary school, I require my students to turn in practice sheets signed by their parents so I can be sure they are putting in enough time. I had to laugh, however, when one parent wrote on her child's sheet, **"Practiced 17 minutes, but it seemed like hours."**

—MEGAN E. TUTTLE

Our school had just installed a new air conditioning system, and a representative from the company wanted to make sure it was running smoothly. Poking his head into an empty classroom, he asked the teacher, "Any little problems here?"

"No," she said, smiling. "All our little problems have gone home."

—ROSALIND POPOV

My wife and I were watching the gorillas at the zoo when several of them charged at the enclosure fence, scattering the crowd, except for one elderly man. Later, my wife asked him how he had kept his composure.

"I used to drive a school bus," he explained.

—MARVYN SAUNDERS

Our architectural school had been without a department chairperson for two years, and students were growing frustrated at the lengthy process of choosing a new candidate. Finally a group of students sent a message to the dean. He arrived at school one morning to find 50 seats stacked up in front of his office. A sign said "Pick a chair!"

—SANDRA HEISER

@@@@@@@@@@@@@@@@@@@@@@@@@@@@@@@@@

I'm a high school geometry teacher and I started one lesson on triangles by reading a theorem. "If an angle is an exterior angle of a triangle, then its measure is greater than the measure of either of its corresponding remote interior angles."

I noticed that one student wasn't taking notes and asked him why.

"Well," he replied sincerely, "I'm waiting until you start speaking English."

—PATRICIA STRICKLAND

After applying their lipstick in the school bathroom, a number of girls would press their lips to the mirror, leaving dozens of little lip prints. The principal decided that something had to be done. So she called all the girls to the bathroom and explained that the lip prints were causing a major problem for the custodian. To demonstrate how difficult it was, she asked the maintenance man to clean one of the mirrors. He took out a long-handled squeegee, dipped it in the toilet and swabbed the glass.

Since then, there have been no lip prints.

—PHIL PROCTOR IN *PLANET PROCTOR*

I was working as a school psychologist in a major city when I was reassigned to a different school. I arrived at my new location early and started to get acquainted with the staff.

The secretary checked for the correct spelling of my name so she could place it on the directory posted near the school entrance.

Later in the day I happened to walk past the directory and saw that she had completed the job, though not in the format I would have expected. There, in front of my name, was the word psycho.

—RICHARD E. BUSEY, JR.

@@@@@@@@@@@@@@@@@@@@@@@@@@@@@@

Rushing to work, I was driving too fast and as a result was pulled over by the highway patrol. The state trooper noticed that my shirt had the name of a local high school on it. "I teach math there," I explained. The trooper smiled, and said, "Okay, here's a problem. A teacher is speeding down the highway at 16 m.p.h. over the limit. At $12 for every mile, plus $40 court costs, plus the rise in her insurance, what's her total cost?" I replied, "Taking that total, subtracting the low salary I receive, multiplying by the number of kids who hate math, then adding to that the fact that none of us would be anywhere without teachers, I'd say zero." He handed me back my license. "Math was never my favorite subject," he admitted. "Please slow down."

—MEGAN STRICKLAND

I'm a teacher and high school basketball coach. During one season, things went from bad to worse when we lost to our local rivals by more than 30 points.

The next day in class, when one of my students asked about the game, I answered, "Let me put it this way. If this were the NBA, I would have been fired today."

"That's not true, Coach," the student said. "If this were the NBA, you would have been fired a long time ago."

—LLOYD ALDRICH

I had been teaching my seventh-graders about World War II, and a test question was, "What was the largest amphibious assault of all time?"

Expecting to see "the D-Day invasion" as the answer, I found instead on one paper, "Moses and the plague of frogs."

—STEVEN CALLAHAN

Last
Laughs

BANANACO PROFITS

"Hard work never killed anybody, but why take a chance?"

—EDGAR BERGEN

@@@@@@@@@@@@@@@@@@@@@@@@@@@@@

Kids' Quips

As a security officer for a defense contractor, I have to make sure all visitors sign in. One day I was in the lobby and noticed an employee's college-age daughter writing in the visitors' log. When I checked the log at the end of the day, I noticed her signature. Next to "Purpose of visit" she had written, "To get money from Dad."

—JOSEPH HOFFLER

I have my office in my home. When family matters occupy my day, I often find myself working into the night to complete business assignments. After one particularly late session, I stood in front of my mirror the next morning applying cover-stick to camouflage the dark circles under my eyes.

"Mom must have been working late last night," I overheard my son telling his siblings. "She's using Wite-Out."

—MARY J. MILLS

On Take Your Daughter to Work Day, I brought my niece to the office with me so she could experience many aspects of being a social worker. While driving her home, I asked if she had learned anything. "Yes," she answered. "I learned that I don't want to do your job."

—KIM RIDER

Trying to explain to our five-year-old daughter how much computers had changed, my husband pointed to our brand-new personal computer and told her that when he was in college, a computer with the same amount of power would have been the size of a house.

Wide-eyed, our daughter asked, "How big was the mouse?"

—CYNDY HINDS

Stopping to pick up my daughter at kindergarten, I found out that the topic of show-and-tell that day had been parents' occupations. The teacher pulled me aside. Whispering, she advised, "You might want to explain a little bit more to your daughter what you do for a living."

I work as a training consultant and often conduct my seminars in motel conference rooms.

When I asked why, the teacher explained, "Your daughter told the class she wasn't sure what you did, but said you got dressed real pretty and went to work at motels."

—MARY BETH NELSEN

My coworker's sweet six-year-old came into the office to sell Girl Scout cookies. A first-year Brownie, she carefully approached each of us and described the various types of cookies. One woman who was struggling with a weight problem asked, "Do you have anything that is not fattening?"

"Yes, ma'am!" the girl brightly answered. "We have Thin Mints!"

—JULIE SANDERS

When shopping online, it's easy to forget that you may not be dealing with a large corporation.

I recently e-mailed a website asking why my purchases hadn't arrived a week after I'd paid for them. Later the phone rang. "Sorry for the delay," said a teenager. "I'll check and get back to you. I can't get on my computer right now because my mother's vacuuming and this room only has one socket."

—TERESA HEWITT

One of my duties as a bookstore supervisor is to handle customer returns. As I helped one young woman, I noticed the book she brought back was on the subject of dating. It's the bookstore's policy to ask the reason for the return, so I did. "My mother bought it for me," she said. "She doesn't like my boyfriend."

—KELLEY MITCHELL

I stole a couple of minutes from work to give my wife a call. She put my two-year-old son on, and we chatted a while before he ended it with an enthusiastic "I love you!"

"I love you too," I said, with a dopey grin plastered on my face. I was about to hang up when I heard him ask sweetly, "Mommy, who was that?"

—MATTHEW TERRY

@@@@@@@@@@@@@@@@@@@@@@@@@@@@@@@

My aunt, a kindergarten teacher, has to interview every new student. During an interview, she asked a little girl what her mother did. The girl proudly replied, "She is a businesswoman."

"What does you father do?" my aunt asked.

After thinking for a moment, the girl said, "He does what my mom tells him to do."

—APA RATTAPITAK

As an optometrist, I had a second-grader in for his first eye exam. He insisted his eyesight was good, but when I asked him to read a line from my vision chart, with the letters APEOTF, he couldn't do it. I asked him about a line with the letters FZBDE, in larger print. Still he couldn't read the chart.

"You mean you can't read those lines," I said, puzzled, "and yet you don't think you need glasses?"

"No," he replied. "I just haven't learned those words yet."

—SEAN CONNOLLY, OD

A student tore into our school office. "My iPod was stolen!" she cried. I handed her a form, and she filled it out, answering everything, even those questions intended for the principal. Under "Disposition," she wrote, "I'm really ticked off."

—DEBORAH MILES

Before my son could start going on job interviews, he needed to dress the part. That, he decided, required a $500 suit.

"What!?" I answered, gagging at the price tag. "I've bought cars for $500!"

"That's why I want the $500 suit," he said. **"So I don't have to drive $500 cars."**

—JOE KULAKOWSKI

At our base post office, my four-year-old could not take his eyes off the Most Wanted posters. Finally, he asked, "Dad, why didn't they just capture those guys when they took their pictures?"

—RAY OSBURN

Carrying mail, I walk the same route every day. One morning a girl was playing outside her house and called out, "Hi, Bill!" Though that isn't my name, I cheerily replied, "Hi!" This went on for several weeks, until I saw the girl's mother and asked, "Why does she call me Bill?"

The mother turned red. "Because whenever I see you coming," she explained, "I tell her, 'Here come the bills.'"

—LINCOLN REHAK

I had signed up to be a school volunteer and was helping a first-grader with her homework. But it turned out I was the one in need of help. The assignment required coloring, and I'm color-blind—can't tell blue from red. As we finished our lesson, I told the little girl, "Next week you can read to me."

Looking confused, she said, "Can't you read, either?"

—HOWARD SIEPLINGA

When my neighbor's teenage son was interviewed for a job at the local discount store, he was asked, "How would you treat an irate customer?"

The boy thought for a moment. "I'd treat him the same as the customer before and the one after."

He was hired on the spot. Later, his mother asked about the interview.

"I guess it went well because I got the job," the son replied. "By the way, Mom, what does 'irate' mean?"

ANN MARIE ROWLANDS

The college football player knew his way around the locker room better than he did the library. So when my husband's coworker saw the gridiron star roaming the stacks looking confused, she asked how she could help.

"I have to read a play by Shakespeare," he said.

"Which one?" she asked.

He scanned the shelves and answered, "William."

—SANDRA J. YARBROUGH

My 17-year-old niece was looking for a job, so her mother scoured the want ads with her. "Here's one. A couple are looking for someone to watch their two kids and do light housekeeping."

"Hellooo!" said my niece, rolling her eyes. "I can't take that job. I don't know anything about lighthouses."

—KIM WILSON

A first-grader came to the ophthalmology office where I work to have his vision checked. He sat down and I turned off the lights. Then I switched on a projector that flashed the letters F, Z and B on a screen. I asked the boy what he saw. Without hesitation he replied, "Consonants."

—STEPHEN DOWNING

Dumb and Dumber

Before setting off on a business trip to Tulsa, I called the hotel where I'd be staying to see if they had a gym. The hotel operator's sigh had a tinge of exasperation in it. "We have over 300 guests at this facility," she said. "Does this 'Gym' have a last name?"

—TARA CAPPADONA

@@@@@@@@@@@@@@@@@@@@@@@@@@@@@

"These are very disturbing figures. So I made all the zeros little smiley faces."

In the deli where I worked, an employee was asked to post a sign advertising our latest meat special. After she put up the sign, however, our manager pointed out that she had listed only the price and needed to put the item on the placard too. Later he was shocked to see a slice of ham taped to the sign.

—SUSAN DYCUS

An elevator in our office building is frequently out of order. The last time, maintenance posted a sign that summed up the situation: Elevator Closed for Temporary Repairs.

—TERRI CRUDUP

Our colleague, a frequenter of pubs, applied for a vanity license plate that would cement his reputation as the "bar king." A week later he arrived to work with his new plates: BARKING.

—NANCY SEND

I needed a passport and I needed it quickly. Luckily, a sign in the passport office told me exactly how long I could expect to wait: "Allow 10 minutes for regular processing and 15 minutes for expedited processing."

—PETER VOGEN

Just as she was celebrating her 80th birthday, our friend received a jury-duty notice. She called to remind the people at the clerk's office that she was exempt because of her age. "You need to come in and fill out the exemption forms," they said.

"I've already done that," replied my friend. "I did it last year."

"You have to do it every year," she was told.

"Why?" came the response. "Do you think I'm going to get younger?"

—JONNIE SIVLEY

It's often a challenge to explain to strangers exactly what I do in the aerospace industry. At one gathering, I didn't even try. I just said, "I'm a defense contractor."

One of the guys was intrigued. "So, what do you put up mainly? Chain-link?"

—JOHN MCGEORGE

@@@@@@@@@@@@@@@@@@@@@@@@@@@@@@@@@

A tree in our front yard was weeping sap, so I visited the office of the U.S. Forest Service for advice. When I explained my problem to a staff member, he stepped to the back of the office and called out, "Anyone here know anything about trees?"

—JIM BRADLEY

The stoplight on the corner buzzes when it's safe to cross the street. I was walking with a coworker of mine, when she asked if I knew what the buzzer was for.

"It signals to blind people when the light is red," I said.

Unhappy with my explanation, she shot back, "What on earth are blind people doing driving?"

—RINKWORKS.COM

In my job with a delivery company, I was getting directions to a customer's home. The woman very specifically said, "From the main road in the center of town go two lights. Look for the bank. Turn right onto the next avenue. Go 1.2 miles. Drive past a yellow hydrant and then take the next left. Go 200 yards. My driveway is the third on the right, and the number is on the mailbox."

As I entered the information into the computer, I asked, "What color is your house?"

The woman paused a second, then said, "Hold on. I'll go check."

—MELISSA A. DOOLEN

A customer called our airline's reservation office to pay for his ticket with a credit card. My coworker asked him, "Would you please spell the name as it appears on the card, sir?"

The customer replied, **"V-I-S-A."**

—CATHY MOSELEY

@@@@@@@@@@@@@@@@@@@@@@@@@@@@@@@@

A customer at the post office called to complain that she hadn't received a package. "Can I have your name and address?" I asked.

"All of that is on the package," she snapped.

"Yes, I know," I replied, "but—"

"Just call me when you find it."

"Can I have your phone number then?"

"I can't remember. But I'm listed," she said, and hung up.

—CHESTER D. STANHOPE

A customer walked into our insurance office looking for a quote. But first I had to lead her through a litany of questions, including: "Marital status?"

"Well," she began, "I guess you could say we're happy—as happy as most other couples nowadays."

—SHIRLEY WALKER

Meeting with my new pastor, I asked if I could have a church service when I eventually die. "Of course," he said, grabbing his date book. "What day do you want?"

—EDITH KRZYWICKI

I was waiting tables in a noisy lobster restaurant in Maine when a vacationing Southerner stumped me with a drink order. I approached the bartender. "Have you ever heard of a drink called 'Seven Young Blondes'?" I asked.

He admitted he'd never heard of it, and grabbed a drink guidebook to look it up. Unable to find the recipe, he then asked me to go back and tell the patron that he'd be happy to make the drink if he could list the ingredients for him. "Sir," I asked the customer, "can you tell me what's in that drink?"

He looked at me like I was crazy. "It's wine," he said, pronouncing his words carefully, "Sauvignon blanc."

—CHRISTIE ECKELS

I was going out to a business lunch with two other people, one of whom volunteered to drive. After the driver unlocked the passenger door, I decided to hop in the back to avoid one of those awkward scenes where you hem and haw over who sits where. But I had trouble getting the seat back to fold forward. I pulled the lever under the seat to slide it forward, but it only moved a few inches.

Not easily discouraged, I hiked up my skirt, and was about to dive into the back when the third member of our party intervened. "Wouldn't it be easier," she said, "just to use the back door?"

—JENNIFER DUFFIN

Working from home as I do, I need a professional-sounding voice-mail greeting so everyone will know I'm hard at work. While I was recording a new message one morning, my wife was across the hall from my office, folding clothes with my six-year-old daughter, who had just emerged from the shower. My message ended up sounding like this:

Male voice: "Hi, this is Jeff Hill with IBM."
Female voice: "Look at you! You have no clothes on!"
Male voice: "I'm not available right now…"

—SUE SHELLENBARGER

When my husband ran for local public office, I was asked if I could do some research on the cost of getting his campaign literature printed up. So I visited a large printing chain to gather pricing information on copying costs. The clerk read off the various prices for color copies, color paper, one-sided printing, two-sided, multiple-color ink, etc.

Since I could not write as fast as the clerk could read, I requested a pricing list. "Sorry, Ma'am," she said. "This is my only copy."

—KAREN ENDRES

"Weston's been watching *Mad Men* again."

At the nature park where I worked in Hawaii, cliff divers often filled in as lifeguards at the falls. On chilly days, however, they wore sweatshirts that covered the lifeguard badges on their swimsuits, so it wasn't apparent that they were safety officers. One day three preteen daredevils ignored my coworker Nancy when she told them not to dive in the pond's shallow edge. Challenging her authority, one boy said in defiance, "Who says?"

"THIS says!" Nancy replied, lifting her sweatshirt to display her lifeguard badge. Seeing their wide-eyed stares and feeling cool air, Nancy only needed a second to remember that she had already removed her wet swimsuit earlier in the day.

—SHIRLEY GERUM

@@@@@@@@@@@@@@@@@@@@@@@@@@@@@@@@

Employee of the Month is a good example of when a person can be a winner and a loser at the same time.

—DEMETRI MARTIN

An absent-minded coworker and I went on a business trip. True to form, he left a book on the plane, arrived at the hotel with someone else's luggage, then lost his camera in a restaurant.

Returning home a week later, we headed to the airport parking lot to get his car, only to discover that he had no keys; he had left them in the trunk lock the week before. Fortunately, someone had turned them in to an attendant. My colleague was driving me home when I noticed the gas tank was empty, so we stopped at a service station. After paying for the gas, he hopped back in the car and drove off. "Promise me that you won't tell anyone at work that I left those keys in the trunk lock," he pleaded. "Okay," I agreed, "as long as I can tell them that you paid for gas and left without pumping it."

—MICHELLE A. BETZEL

Our intern was not very swift. One day, he turned to a secretary. "I'm almost out of typing paper. What do I do?"

"Just use copy-machine paper," she said to him.

With that, the intern took his last remaining piece of blank typing paper, put it in the photocopier and proceeded to make five blank copies.

As a salesperson, I do a lot of business over the phone. One man who called to place an order had a nice voice, so when he asked if I wanted his number, I took the opportunity to offer mine as well.

"Um," he stammered, "I was talking about my purchase-order number."

—IRIS MADDEROM

As a personal-injury attorney, I often get clients who have unsuccessfully attempted to settle their claims themselves. During a phone interview one woman told me that having lived on both coasts, she was more than capable of handling her claim, but the insurance company was giving her trouble. "Where did the accident occur?" I asked.

When she answered "Washington," I inquired, "Washington State or Washington, D.C.?"

There was a slight pause. "Hold on," she said. "I'll check the police report."

—CHRISTOPHER J. CARNEY

My daughter attends Oregon State University and works part time at a grocery store. With the holidays approaching, she worried about having enough time to study for finals, so she penned a memo to her manager. "It is absolutely imperative that I receive four days off," she wrote. "Otherwise I will not have time to study."

The next day her request was tacked to the employee bulletin board along with a note from her boss. "If I allow these days off," read the reply, "it is absolutely imperative that I know who you are."

—JANEY POWERS

When a client died, her daughter told our agency that she would cancel the home policy the following week, once her mother's belongings were removed.

Simple, right? Here's the note that was placed in the client's file: **"Deceased will call next week to cancel moving her things out."**

—KARLA WYNDER

Working as a server at a sushi bar, I saw a customer trying to get my attention. "What's up, babe?" he asked in a strong foreign accent. "Everything is fine, sir," I replied. After a while the patron hailed me again, asking "What's up, babe?" Puzzled and annoyed, I gave the same reply. Observing this was my supervisor, who called me over. "What did that customer ask?" he inquired. When I told him, he smiled. "He doesn't want to know how you're doing," my boss said with a laugh. "He's asking for wasabi!"

—VIJAY KRISHAN

"I don't dare leave my desk, dear. Ferguson's waiting to pounce on my job."

@@@@@@@@@@@@@@@@@@@@@@@@@@@@@@

While auditing one of our departments, an assistant asked me what I was doing. "Listing your assets," I told her.

"Oh," she said. "Well, I have a good sense of humor and I make great lasagna."

—ALEC KAY

I was on the phone at the end of the day when my boss walked in and pressed a sticky note onto a nearby filing cabinet. I had already put away my glasses and was in a rush to leave, so I quickly scanned the slip of paper and called after him, "I have feelings for you, too!"

He looked back at me quizzically and was gone. Then I took a closer look at the note. It read, "I have filing for you."

—MELODY DELZELL

Tourists say some odd things when they charter my boat in Key West. "How many sunset sails do you have at night?" asked one. Another wondered, "Does the water go around the island?"

But the most interesting came when I asked a customer why she'd brought along a dozen empty jars. She answered, "I want to take home a sample of each color of water that we'll be going in."

—DENISE JACKSON

As an amusement-park employee, I am often asked for directions to specific attractions. Although detailed maps are given to each customer who enters the park, some people need more help. One exasperated guest approached me after she'd gotten lost using the map. "How come these maps don't have an arrow telling you where you are?" she asked.

—J. B. HAIGHT

@@@@@@@@@@@@@@@@@@@@@@@@@@@@@@@@

Here's an ad for a job that should be filled quickly:
"Animal Hospital is seeking an Assistant.
Must be flexible, reliable, and irresponsible."

—MARGERY JOHNSON

A blonde was settling into a first-class seat for a flight to Los Angeles when the flight attendant asked to see her ticket. "Ma'am, you can't sit here," the attendant explained. "You have a coach ticket."

"I'm blond, I'm beautiful, and I'm going to Los Angeles first-class," the blond passenger declared.

So the flight attendant went to get her supervisor, who explained, "I'm sorry, but you'll have to move to coach because you don't have a first-class ticket."

"I'm blond, I'm beautiful, and I'm going to Los Angeles first-class," repeated the gorgeous young blonde.

The two attendants went to the cockpit and told the captain. He came back and whispered something to the blonde. She jumped up and quickly took a seat in the coach section. Astounded, the flight attendants asked the captain what he had said. "I told her that first class wasn't going to Los Angeles," he replied.

—CORY CAMPBELL

A friend stopped at a convenience store, but the automatic doors wouldn't open. Thinking there was an electronic eye, he began to wave his arms. An employee inside the store waved back. My friend then wedged his fingers between the sliding glass doors and created an opening wide enough to enter. "Your doors are out of order!" he hollered to a clerk. "Why didn't you help me?"

"Sir," he replied, "we're closed!"

—KEVIN J. SHANNON

At the funeral home where my husband works, the funeral director asked a recent widower, "Did your wife's illness come out of the blue?"

"No, she'd been sick before," he said. "But never this bad."

—JACKIE WISSMUELLER

While working in a clothing store, I noticed that people had no shame about returning items that obviously had been worn. One rainy morning I walked in and found a discolored blazer hanging on the rack with other returns. "People return the most filthy, nasty things," I commented to my supervisor who was standing nearby.

Eyebrow raised, she said, "That's my jacket."

—JOYCE A. WATTS

A fellow nurse at my hospital received a call from an anxious woman. "I'm diabetic and I'm afraid I've had too much sugar today," she said.

"Are you lightheaded?" my colleague asked.

"No, I'm a brunette."

—PAM FORST

Plate-glass windows cover the front of the office where I work. One day a military plane on maneuvers caused a sonic boom that cracked one of the windows. My boss called the local air base to file a claim and was finally transferred to a woman who handled such matters. After she carefully asked him the pertinent details of the incident, she had one final question: **"Did you get the ID number off the plane?"**

—MICHELLE BURTON

@@@@@@@@@@@@@@@@@@@@@@@@@@@@@@

A customer called our service line demanding help with her TV set, which wouldn't come on.

"I'm sorry, but we can't send a technician out today due to the blizzard," I told her.

Unsatisfied, she barked, "I need my TV fixed today! What else am I supposed to do while the power is out?!"

—ARIELLE MOBLEY

Our new assistant, Christy, 16, was in her first office job. Coworkers were giving her basic instructions as the boss stepped out of his office and the telephone rang. Christy answered professionally, but then burst out with, "He's in the restroom now."

"Oh, no," one employee whispered to her. "Say he's with a customer."

"He's in the restroom with a customer," Christy told the caller.

—JIM OTTS

As I was waiting for my wife at the reception desk at a spa, a flustered woman entered. She apologized to the receptionist for being late. "I walked up and down both sides of the street for 15 minutes trying to find the entrance to the spa," she said. When she finished her explanation, the receptionist's first question was, "Have you ever been here before?"

—ED SWARTZACK

During a conference, I was pleasantly surprised to be seated next to a very handsome man. We flirted casually through dinner, then grew restless as the dignitaries gave speeches. During one particularly long-winded lecture, my new friend drew a # sign on a cocktail napkin. Elated, I wrote down my phone number. Looking startled for a moment, he drew another # sign, this time adding an *X* to the upperleft-hand corner.

—KARI MOORE

"The plan is to re-establish confidence in my leadership abilities."

Following the birth of my second child, I called our insurance company to inquire about my short-term disability policy.

"I just had a baby," I proudly announced to the representative who picked up the phone.

"Congratulations! I'll get all of your information and activate your policy," she assured me. After taking down basic facts like my name and address, she asked, "Was this a work-related incident?"

—HEIDI TOURSIE

@@@@@@@@@@@@@@@@@@@@@@@@@@@@@@@@

My colleague used to work as a receptionist at an upscale salon. After greeting clients, she would ask them to change into a protective gown.

One afternoon a serious-looking businessman entered the salon, and was directed to the changing room and told the gowns were hanging on the hooks inside. Minutes later he emerged.

"I'm ready," he called out. My friend gasped. Instead of a gown, the man was wearing something another client had left hanging in the room—a floral blouse with shoulder pads.

—SHERRIE GRAHAM

Standing in line in a hardware store, I noted a woman looking at a rack full of signs priced at $1.79 each. She took one out and put it back a couple of times. Suddenly she held up the sign that read "Help Wanted," and asked the clerk, "Is there a discount on the sign if it's just going over the kitchen sink?"

—NANCY M. BAUMANN

An art lover stopped by my booth at a crafts fair to admire one of my paintings.

"Is that a self-portrait?" he asked.

"Yes, it is," I said.

"Who did it?"

—FLORENCE KAUFMAN

The secret to why librarians spend their days shushing people. Here are actual questions asked of librarians:

- "Can you tell me why so many Civil War battles were fought in national parks?"

- "Do you have any books with photos of dinosaurs?"

- "I need to find out Ibid's first name for my bibliography."

@@@@@@@@@@@@@@@@@@@@@@@@@@@@@@

A sign outside a nursery: "It's spring!
We're so excited, we wet our plants!"

—BECKY ADAIR

Applying for my first passport, I took all the relevant
papers to the passport desk at the post office. The clerk checked
over my application form, photos, marriage license, and other
identification. All seemed in order until she came to my birth
certificate. She handed it back to me and said, "This isn't any
good. It's in your maiden name."

—JACQUELYN S. CAIN

A woman called the county office where I work and asked me
to look up a "Mark Smith."
   "Is that 'Mark' with a 'C' or 'K'?" I asked.
   "That's 'Mark' with an 'M,'" she corrected.

—ANN KEKAHUNA

When a body was brought to her funeral home, my friend
contacted the next of kin. Per previous instructions, the deceased
would be cremated, she told him, so he needed to come in to
identify the body.
   Considering the task at hand, the relative asked, "Does this
need to be done before or after the cremation?"

—JANICE PIERSON

When a water main broke, a customer called my friend at the
utility office with this question: **"The water in my toilet is
brown. Do you think it's safe to drink?"**

—DAVID KEGLEY

"Hargett is still adjusting from working at home."

Every couple of months I do a bulk mailing for my company, which requires a special form from the U.S. Postal Service. I had a faxed copy of the form that was illegible, so I phoned the post office and asked the postal employee to mail me a new form. "I can fax you the form but I can't mail it to you," she replied. "We no longer send mail from this post office."

—CHRISTY ADAMS

Just for Laughs

"**A** recession," claimed the stockbroker, "is when your neighbor loses his job. A depression is when you lose your job. And panic is when your wife loses her job."

—WINSTON K. PENDLETON

In my role as a human resources officer, I was visited by a staff member who wanted to make a formal complaint about his line manager. The boss had described him as "indecisive", which he felt was grossly unfair.

As I was helping him prepare his case, I noticed that the appraisal was almost a year old.

"Why has it taken so long for you to come and see me?" I asked.

"Well," he said. "I couldn't make up my mind if it was the right thing to do or not."

—ALEC KAY

My musical director wasn't happy with the performance of one of our percussionists. Repeated attempts to get the drummer to improve failed. Finally, in front of the orchestra, the director said in frustration, "When a musician just can't handle his instrument, they take it away, give him two sticks and make him a drummer!"

A stage whisper was heard from the percussion section: "And if he can't handle that, they take away one of his sticks and make him a conductor."

—QUINN WONG

My nephew gave up his lucrative job to become a writer. "Have you sold anything yet?" I asked him one day.

"Yes," he said. "My car and my television."

—PATRICK DICKINSON

@@@@@@@@@@@@@@@@@@@@@@@@@@@@@@@@

After earning my degree in broadcast journalism, I was fortunate to land a job as a disc jockey at a top-rated local radio station. One day before work, I stopped by my parents' house, where my mother was chatting with some friends. She introduced me to everyone and proudly mentioned that I had my own radio show. "How is it having a son who's a popular radio personality?" asked one friend. "It's wonderful!" Mom replied with glee. "For the first time in his life, I can turn him off whenever I please."

—TERRY ERHARDT

Near St. Vincent's Hospital in New York City I noticed two firefighters standing at the door of their ambulance. The window was partly down, and they were talking to a small child inside, instructing her how to open the latch. Nearby, a young mother looked on patiently.

Assuming they had invited the curious girl into the ambulance to check it out and she'd locked the doors by mistake, I said, "She locked herself in, eh?"

"No, we locked ourselves out," one of the men said. "We borrowed her from her mom because she fit through the back window."

—GILBERT ROGIN IN *THE NEW YORK TIMES*

A friend's daughter worked part-time in his office while she attended graduate school. One morning, a call came in for her. "She's not in yet," my friend said. "Can I take a message?"

"I'll call back later," the woman answered.

At 11 o'clock, she tried again, and he reported that his daughter had gone to lunch.

The last call came at 3:30. "Sorry, she's left for the day. Anything I can help you with?"

"Yes," the caller replied. "How can I get a job with you?"

—JOSH PATE

@@@@@@@@@@@@@@@@@@@@@@@@@@@@@@@

A small display at the fish hatchery where I work describes a now-extinct fish called the Michigan grayling. Last summer, I had the following conversation with a tourist:

Tourist: Is the grayling still extinct?
Me: Yes, sir. It no longer exists.
Tourist: Any thoughts of bringing it back?
Me: I don't think that's possible.
Tourist: Why not?
Me: Because it's extinct.
Tourist: Still?

—RINKWORKS.COM

Every time my construction crew began pouring a concrete foundation, our foreman would repeatedly warn us not to drop any tools into the mixture because we'd never get them out. During one particularly hard job, a coworker asked the foreman how many more minutes it would be until our break. "I really don't know," he replied sheepishly, looking down at the foundation we had just poured. "I dropped my watch in there over an hour ago."

—BRAD VICTOR

I'd just lobbied a Congressman in his Washington, D.C., office when I stopped to use the rest room. After washing my hands, I stepped up to the hand dryer and noticed a note pasted to it. The note said **"Push button for message from Congress."**

—MICHAEL BROKOVICH

@@@@@@@@@@@@@@@@@@@@@@@@@@@@@@@@

Light bulb jokes are an innocent way to poke fun—or so I thought. Working as a sound technician, I asked an electrician, who was also the local union steward: "Hey, Mike. How many Teamsters does it take to change a light bulb?" (I expected the classic answer: "Twelve. You got a problem with that?") But Mike replied in all seriousness, "None. Teamsters shouldn't be touching light bulbs."

—TODD PILON

While my fellow "financial services representatives" and I were making phone calls one day, I noticed a colleague bristle at something the business owner at the other end of the line had said. Later, when I asked him what had happened, he frowned. "She called me an insurance agent," he said, obviously taking offense at the negative stereotypes that go along with that title.

"Don't kid yourself," I told him. "You are an insurance agent."

"No I'm not!" he replied hotly. "I'm a telemarketer!"

—URI ONDRAS

As a writer for one of the less glamorous sections of a newspaper, I also do entertainment features on rare occasions. Once, I was assigned to review a play that hadn't opened yet. After the rehearsal, I was chatting with the cast and mentioned what I usually do at the paper.

One thespian, shaking his head, remarked, "Oh, great. The play hasn't even opened yet, and they send in the obituary writer."

—ERIKA ENIGK

When he blew a wad of money at my blackjack table in the casino, a customer stood up and yelled, "How do you lose $200 at a $2 table?!"

Before I could speak, another customer replied, "Patience."

—ROBERT GENTRY

@@@@@@@@@@@@@@@@@@@@@@@@@@@@

Project Plan

Procrastinate — panic

WARP

The large fire department where I work sometimes runs out of the official forms we use for inspecting equipment. Headquarters will then allow us to create our own forms on the station's computer.

Once, after composing a replacement document, we sent copies to other fire stations in need of them.

Afterward, we noticed that under the signature line, someone had mistakenly typed "Singed."

—ALBERT LEGGS

Our supervisor recently made a casual comment about my shaggy mane. He then went on to extol the virtues of a good haircut, which, he insisted, makes an elderly man look younger, and a younger man seem more mature.

"How would a haircut make a middle-aged man like me appear?" I asked, trying to stump him.

"Still employed," he answered.

—BRIAN CHEN

A bar in our neighborhood got lots of interesting traffic. Cars swerved into the parking lot, and the drivers would run inside only to reappear minutes later looking confused. One reason might have been the sign outside: "Free Beer, Topless Bartenders, and False Advertising."

—MARKIE REICHERT

A young man hired by a supermarket reported for his first day of work. The manager greeted him with a warm handshake and a smile, gave him a broom and said, "Your first job will be to sweep out the store."

"But I'm a college graduate," the young man replied indignantly.

"Oh, I'm sorry. I didn't know that," said the manager. "Here, give me the broom—I'll show you how."

—RICHARD L. WEAVER II

I returned home from my ninth business trip of the year with a severe bout of jet lag–induced foot-in-mouth disease. As we prepared to go to sleep that night, I wrapped my arms around my better half, gave her a kiss, and announced, **"It's good to be in my own bed, with my own wife!"**

—MARIO NASTASI

@@@@@@@@@@@@@@@@@@@@@@@@@@@@@@@@

Cashier: And what form of payment will you be using today?
Customer: Money.

—OVERHEADINTHEOFFICE.COM

Expenses were out of control at our data supply company, and our bosses weren't happy. "When you travel," the vice president said in a meeting with his sales force, "lunch can't be expensed. Lunch is a normal employee cost. And while we're on the topic, your dinner expenses have been way too high." A rep shouted, "That's because we don't eat lunch."

—CHARLES FENDER

At the Social Security office, I eavesdropped on an interview between a staffer and someone who was applying for benefits.
Staffer: Married or single?
Applicant: Single.
Staffer: Previous marriages?
Applicant: Two.
Staffer: Did either of them end in death?
Applicant: No. Both times I got out alive.

—JOHN K. COLE

I received a letter saying I would not be given the American Express credit card I'd requested because my income wasn't substantial enough. Oddly enough, I work for American Express.

"Do you want to insure this?" asked the clerk at the post office when I handed her my package.
"Nope," I answered. "The contents aren't breakable."
The clerk wasn't so sure. "Ma'am, we are professionals. We can break anything."

—CYNTHIA FRANKLIN

The day before our office's new computer was to arrive, we got a call: the machine wouldn't be ready until the following week. Delays continued. Finally, more than a month later a computer arrived—the wrong model. Office management, however, decided to accept it.

Weeks later, a package came with a letter from the computer dealer, apologizing for the inconvenience. To show that they valued our business, they asked us to accept the enclosed VCR. It was a CD player.

—LYNDON OLFERT

"This performance evaluation is getting weird, sir."

@@@@@@@@@@@@@@@@@@@@@@@@@@@@@@@@@@

While I was handling the reception desk at a women's magazine, the children of several employees sat in the adjoining conference room watching an action video. Trucks screeched, horns honked, people shouted, dogs barked, and cars collided. Just then, a bike messenger arrived to drop off a package. He listened to the cacophony emanating from the conference room, and sighed, "Ah, the soundtrack to my life."

—CHRISTINE ROBERTS IN *THE NEW YORK TIMES*

After I took a job at a small publishing house, the first books I was assigned to edit were all on the topic of dieting. "Isn't the market flooded with these types of books?" I asked another editor. "How do we expect to turn a profit?"

"Don't worry," he assured me. "These books appeal to a wider audience than most."

—WILL STEVENS

The pressure of a workday can bring out the weirdness in people. Possibilities for stupidity are endless. Just check out these chats from overheardintheoffice.com:

Boss: You make too many mistakes! You're not very consistent.

Cube Dweller: Well, you can't be consistent all the time.

—OVERHEADINTHEOFFICE.COM

I work for a mortgage company where I verify financial information about home buyers. One day I was processing a loan for a psychic reader and needed to confirm his income. In response to my request, I received the following letter from his employer: "He is a subcontractor for our psychic readers group. He is not a salaried employee. We therefore cannot predict his future earnings."

—VINCENT A. PATTI

@@@@@@@@@@@@@@@@@@@@@@@@@@@@@@@

When I drove up to the front of our small post office, I was surprised to see plywood covering the area where the plate-glass window used to be. Pasted on the plywood was a sign: "Please leave your car outside."

—AMY DIETZ

While getting dressed one morning, I decided I'd been spending too much time on my computer: I caught myself checking the lower right corner of my makeup mirror to see what time it was.

—DARLENE JACOBS

Corporations' lunch time seminars tend to run long. At one particular company, employees need a supervisor's okay to attend. This led to an interesting memo: "Next Lunch and Learn topic: Who's Controlling Your Life? (Get your manager's permission before attending.)"

—LUKE SECOR

A friend of mine plays piano in a local restaurant. One night, I listened to him play "Send in the Clowns," one of my favorite songs. As he finished, a woman approached him.

"Can you play "Send in the Clowns?" she asked.

My friend shook his head sadly and replied, "Apparently not."

—ERIC LANE BARNES

My husband and I attended a bridal fair trying to drum up work for his fledgling wedding photography business. One vendor assumed we were engaged and asked when the big day was.

"Oh, we've been married ten years," I said.

"Really?" she asked. "But you look so happy."

—IONA DORSEY

QUOTABLE QUOTES

"I always arrive late at the office, but I make up for it by leaving early."

—CHARLES LAMB

"Nothing bad can happen if you haven't hit the Send key."

—DAVID SHIPLEY AND WILL SCHWALBE IN *SEND*

Dennis Miller defines body piercing: "A powerful, compelling visual statement that says 'Gee, in today's competitive job market, what can I do to make myself even less employable?'"

—DENNIS MILLER

"His insomnia was so bad, he couldn't sleep during office hours."

—ARTHUR BAER

"Every day I get up and look through the Forbes list of the richest people in America. If I'm not there, I go to work."

—ROBERT ORBEN

"A raise is like a martini: it elevates the spirit, but only temporarily."

—DAN SELIGMAN

"Eighty percent of success is showing up."

—WOODY ALLEN

"I used to work at the unemployment office. I hated it because when they fired me, I had to show up at work anyway."

—WALLY WANG

"You go to your TV to turn your brain off. You go to the computer when you want to turn your brain on."

—STEVE JOBS

"I do not like work, even when somebody else is doing it."

—MARK TWAIN

@@@@@@@@@@@@@@@@@@@@@@@@@@@@@@

One night, I stopped my city bus and picked up a drunk woman and her male companion. While the guy sat down in the back near two other men, she regaled me with stories about the great birthday party she'd just had. Finally, she went to take a seat but came back seconds later.

"Umm ..." she whispered. "Do you remember which guy I got on the bus with?"

—RICHARD SAWCHIN

Back when I was employed by the state of Michigan, I took a call from an angry worker.

Caller: "Do you know there are no doors on the toilets at our office?"

Me: "How long has this been going on?"

Caller: "At least three months."

Me: "I can see your problem."

Caller: "So can everybody else."

—JAYNIE WELLS

The receptionist for the company where I'm employed found some cash in the office, apparently mislaid by a coworker.

She sent the following e-mail: "If anybody can say where they lost $66, please let me know and it will be returned to you."

Within minutes one employee replied, "Kentucky Derby, 1986."

—MILLIE STEELE

Recently a young woman came into my father's insurance office with her newborn twins.

Dad asked her if she ever had any trouble telling them apart.

She gave him a funny look before responding, "No, I haven't had any problem. This is Benjamin and this is Elizabeth."

—BARB MICHEL

"Mitchell, it's not the fact you found religion that bothers me..."

At our busy stock brokerage, it's hard to find time for small talk. So I was caught off guard when a coworker leaned over to me and asked, "What's up, John?" Welcoming a brief break, I told him about my hectic weekend and the trouble I was having with my car. He seemed a little distracted, however. After our conversation ended, I saw him lean over to another colleague. "Hey, Robert," he said. "What's the ticker symbol for 'Upjohn' pharmaceuticals?"

—JOHN F. HUNT

@@@@@@@@@@@@@@@@@@@@@@@@@@@@@@

After someone stole my brown-bag lunch at work,
I complained about it to my wife, who offered to make me
something wonderful the next day. But as I pulled into
the plant's parking lot, I noticed a guy clearly down
on his luck, so I gave him my lunch. I didn't know
there was a note from my wife in the bag:

"I know who you are, and I know where you live!"

—FRANKLIN BENNETT

Rushing from the parking lot into my office in Los Angeles, I was approached by a homeless man.

"Excuse me, can you spare some change?" he asked.

In a hurry but not wanting to be rude, I pretended I didn't understand him. "No hablo inglés," I replied.

"Oh, that's just great," the guy muttered, as he turned to walk away. "Now you even have to be bilingual to beg."

—ANA TURNER

I was vacationing in the South Carolina mountains with a friend who's a freelance journalist for a couple of small-town newspapers. When she got a call about a car running off a curve and going off the side of the mountain, we hurried to the site. Thankfully no one was hurt. After a quick scan of the spectators, my friend sought out one local man to interview. "Have you lived in this area long?" she asked him. He told her that he had lived here all his life.

Then she asked, "How often do cars go over the side of the mountains?"

"Only once, ma'am," he replied.

—SHARON MCNEIL

When our U.S. corporation was acquired by a European company, I was asked to work with a team of overseas consultants who would determine the future of our business. I was thrilled by the assignment, thinking it was a great opportunity to be noticed by the new corporate management team. For weeks I was at their beck and call, taking pains to provide them with all the data they needed.

One morning while I was working feverishly, the head consultant stepped into my office. "I understand that you are the key expert here," he said as he shook my hand.

Flattered by such recognition, I thanked him and launched into a description of all the effort I had expended.

"You don't understand," he interrupted, holding up a key. "I can't unlock my office door."

—DAVID BAHR

Some of my coworkers and I decided to remove the small, wooden suggestion box from our office because it had received so few entries. We stuck the box on top of a seven-foot-high metal storage cabinet and then promptly forgot about it.

Months later, when the box was moved during remodeling, we found a single slip of paper inside. The suggestion read "Lower the box!"

—FRANK J. MONACO

A coworker in our California office flew to Chicago during a blizzard. He spent hours driving to make his appointment at a suburban office complex. The parking lot was empty, so he pulled up next to the main entrance. As he was signing in, the reception-ist looked outside and asked, **"Before your meeting, could you move your car off the front lawn?"**

—RUSSELL G. GRAHAM

**"A book on male sensitivity?
Try the Fiction Section, aisle two."**

During my first trip to Japan, I was taken to a local restaurant. I had been counseled to try everything on my plate so as not to insult my Japanese hosts. They, in turn, were told to be patient with my American mannerisms. Therefore they said nothing as I crunched my way through a tasteless wafer served with my meal. Later I realized we had all taken the advice too far: I had eaten a coaster.

—LAURA PUCHER

I've been hauling trash for years, so when the sign "Garbage" appeared on a trash can, I replaced it with my own note: "After 20 years on the job, I know garbage when I see it!" I emptied the can and left.

The next week, a new note appeared on the same can: "Dear Professor Trash, the garbage can is the garbage!"

—STAN GORSKI

Scene: A phone conversation between a client and me—an art director.

Me: Hi. I was wondering if you received the invoice I sent?

Client: Yes, I received it, but I am not going to pay you yet.

Me: Why not? Was something wrong?

Client: No, I don't need to use your design yet, so I will pay you when I use it.

Me: Well, I still need to get paid now. If a plumber fixes your toilet, you don't tell him you will pay him as soon as you need to go to the bathroom, do you?

Client: That's disgusting! My bathroom habits are none of your business, and as soon as I use what you sent me, you will get paid!

—FROM CLIENTSFROMHELL.NET

It was Halloween night when a driver called our road-service dispatch office complaining that he was locked out of his car. I forwarded the information to a locksmith, along with one more detail: The car was parked at a nudist colony.

Of course, the locksmith arrived in record time. But when he called in later, he wasn't amused.

"Figures," he said. "I finally get to go to a nudist colony, and they're having a costume party!"

—NEIL KLEIN

@@@@@@@@@@@@@@@@@@@@@@@@@@@@@@@

A Rochester, N.Y., firm posted a notice announcing it would pay $100 to anyone who came up with an idea that could save the company money immediately. The first winner was an employee who suggested that the award be cut to $50.

—EXECUTIVE SPEECHWRITER NEWSLETTER

The day I started my construction job, I was in the office filling out an employee form when I came to the section that asked: Single____, Married____, Divorced____.

I marked single. Glancing at the man next to me, who was also filling out his form, I noticed he hadn't marked any of the blanks. Instead he'd written, "Yes, in that order."

—BECQUET.COM

The company I work for recently purchased a building that had once been a hospital. Management asked for volunteers to help with some light renovation. I joined up, and my first task was to take signs down in the parking lot.

One read, "Reserved for Physician." I said to a coworker that I should keep the sign and post it on my sister's garage door. My friend asked, "Is your sister a doctor?"

"No," I replied. "She's single."

—JOHN ALLEN

While driving through South Carolina, I kept on having to slow down for road repair crews.

To keep the workers safe, the highway department posted a series of signs that read, "Let 'em work. Let 'em live."

On one of the signs an exasperated motorist had added, **"Let 'em finish!"**

—JOYCE BURDETT

I arrived at the office early one morning and noticed someone had left the lid to the copy machine open. I closed the lid and settled in for the workday. Over the next few weeks I found someone was continually leaving the lid up. Finally I caught the guilty party, surprised I hadn't figured out who it was long before. The culprit was Richard—the only male on our staff.

—TRUDY M. GALLMAN

My friend, a grocery store manager, chased a shoplifter through dry goods and frozen foods before catching the perp with a leaping tackle in cleaning supplies. That's when my friend noticed that all of the customers in line at the cash registers were staring.

"Everything's fine, folks," he assured them. "This guy just tried to go through the express lane with more than ten items."

—PAT PATEL

A famous scientist was on his way to yet another lecture when his chauffeur offered an idea. "Hey, boss, I've heard your speech so many times, I bet I could deliver it and give you the night off."

"Sounds great," the scientist said.

When they got to the auditorium, the scientist put on the chauffeur's hat and settled into the back row. The chauffeur walked to the lectern and delivered the speech. Afterward he asked if there were any questions.

"Yes," said one professor. Then he launched into a highly technical question.

The chauffeur was panic-stricken for a moment but quickly recovered. "That's an easy one," he replied. "So easy, I'm going to let my chauffeur answer it."

—KUMIKO YOSHIDA

When flooding closed the pressroom at a U.S. government office last spring, a spokeswoman remarked, "This is the first time that a leak has stopped the press from writing."

—RONALD G. SHAFER IN *THE WALL STREET JOURNAL*

I'm a mechanic who was called to help a stranded motorist. When I arrived, the woman was telling her car, "C'mon" as she tried to start it. She said that the car belonged to one of her children, and that she didn't know what was wrong with it. I suspected the engine was flooded, so I waited a few minutes before trying the ignition again. Then I, too, said "C'mon" as I turned the key. The vehicle started immediately.

"Great," said the woman. "Not only don't my kids listen to me, but they've trained their cars not to listen to me either."

—JOHN PUSHKO

At the bank where I was employed as a teller we were not allowed to eat while working. But one day, five months pregnant, I was ravenous. I opened a bag of potato chips and started to devour them.

Just then I spotted one of our best customers and his wife heading my way. Quickly, I wiped my mouth and greeted them. As I processed their transaction, I noticed they were looking at me oddly.

On their way out, the man said, "I don't understand these young people."

"Dear, that's a fashion statement," his wife explained. "It's a new type of brooch."

I looked down to see what could have caused such controversy. To my horror, a large potato chip was resting neatly on my left shoulder.

—JOANN MANNIX

@@@@@@@@@@@@@@@@@@@@@@@@@@@@@@@@

Conductor Sir Neville Marriner was leading the Boston Symphony at Tanglewood, in Massachusetts. During the final chords of the program many concert-goers would leave their seats so they could beat the traffic. When asked if he was irritated, Marriner reacted with English aplomb. No, he said, he preferred to think that he was being rewarded with "a standing evacuation."

—MICHAEL RYAN

As personnel assistant for a printing company, I had to update the job descriptions and asked various managers for their input. When the controller, the owner's son, returned a form I had distributed, the section entitled "job qualifications" was left blank. I sent it back and asked that he complete the form. He did, adding this reply: "Must be related to the boss and have an accounting degree from Notre Dame."

—JANET PETZNICK

"That's two 'ayes', two 'nays' and one 'whatever.'"

Late for work already, I was annoyed to find a strange car in my reserved parking space again. After locating a spot far away, I stormed into my office determined to have the car towed. As the morning wore on, however, my anger mellowed and I decided to give the driver another chance.

During lunchtime, I went outside and left this note on the driver's windshield: "Please don't take my parking space. If you do, and your car disappears, don't say I never towed you!"

—LARRY HOUPT

Scanning the phone book for a garbage collection service, I came across one that clearly wasn't afraid to tackle any job. Their ad read: "Residential hauling. All types of junk removed. No load too large or too small. Garages, basements, addicts."

—MARY BETH CARROLL

At the hardware store where I work, our manager was writing out a bill when he turned to me and asked, "Hey, what are these nuts worth?"

A new clerk looked up and said,
"I thought we were getting seven bucks an hour."

—DENNIS SCARROW

The new city hall in Chandler, Arizona, is eco-friendly and uses recycled gray water in the toilets. Just to be safe, a sign went up in the bathrooms warning employees not to drink out of the toilets. "I'm glad I saw that sign because I was very thirsty," deadpanned the mayor.

—AZCENTRAL.COM

Getting into my car one night, I turned the key and was dismayed to discover that the battery was dead. I took out my cell phone and dialed the automobile club. Just as the dispatcher answered, there was a loud fender bender on the highway nearby.

"Wow," the dispatcher said, hearing the crunch of metal on metal. **"Most people wait until after the accident to call."**

—TIM O'BRIEN

The large office building that I work in is showing signs of its advanced age. Structural and cosmetic renovations began well over two years ago, and no end is in sight. The chronic chaos moves unpredictably from floor to floor.

The tenants apparently are feeling the stress. Posted in the elevator one morning was a hand-lettered warning sign left by the workmen: "Watch your step—floors 3, 4, and 5." By lunchtime, someone had added, "have been removed."

—CAROLE M. SAMPECK

Ernest, my husband, was playing golf with our town's fire chief when he hit a ball into the rough. As Ernest headed for the brush to find his ball, the chief warned, "Be careful, the rattlesnakes are out."

The chief explained that calls had been coming in all week requesting assistance with removing the snakes.

"You've got to be kidding," Ernest replied in astonishment. "People actually call you to help them with rattlesnakes? What do you say to them?"

"Well," said the chief, "the first thing I ask is, 'Is it on fire?'"

—LAURA PETERSON

"It's $50 for fixing the sink, and $300 for babysitting your husband."

I owned a taxi service with my husband, William. While sitting in a cab waiting for a fare, William saw that a downpour had left puddles stretching to the curb. Then he heard someone open the back door and get in. When he turned around to ask the destination, William saw the would-be passenger exiting the other door. "Thanks," said the passenger. "I just wanted to get over the water."

—MARY SPROULE

Being in the bee removal business, I'm used to frantic phone calls, like the one from the woman whose home was infested with bees.

"You don't understand," she said, explaining why she was so upset. "I have two small children here."

"I do understand," I reassured her. "I have six children of my own."

"Oh," she said, now calmer. "I guess you don't have the 'birds' part down yet."

—KAY JONES

My budget-minded mother is always clipping coupons and keeps detailed records of how much money she saves. One day while running the cash register at the drugstore where she works, she had a self-conscious young man approach the counter to buy some condoms. My mother noticed a dollar-off coupon on the box and asked him if he'd like to use it, adding that she and her husband had saved over $400 redeeming coupons last year.

The stunned young man replied, "On these?"

—ELAINE EHRCKE STARNES

On my first day at the gas station, I watched a coworker measure the level of gasoline in the underground tanks by lowering a giant measuring stick down into them.

"What would happen if I threw a lit match into the hole?" I joked.

"It would go out," he answered very matter-of-factly.

"Really?" I asked, surprised to hear that. "Is there a safety device that would extinguish it before the fumes are ignited?"

"No," my coworker replied. "The force from the explosion would blow the match out."

—DAN WALTER

At the large bookstore where my son works, the clerks tend to watch out for one another, trading shifts and covering for each other in emergencies. Recently, though, a disagreement between two clerks escalated into a fistfight. One of them ended up going to the hospital, leaving my son to cover for him.

The store manager, who had missed the whole episode, later came looking for the injured clerk. "Where's Jack?" the man asked.

My son didn't miss a beat. "Oh," he said, "he punched out early."

—ELLEN KAHN

I'm a counselor who helps coordinate support groups for visually impaired adults. Many participants have a condition known as macular degeneration, which makes it difficult for them to distinguish facial features.

I had just been assigned to a new group and was introducing myself.

Knowing that many in the group would not be able to see me very well, I jokingly said, "For those of you who can't see me, I've been told that I look like a cross between Paul Newman and Robert Redford."

Immediately one woman called out, "We're not that blind!"

—BOB SHANKLAND

Neither snow, nor rain, nor heat, nor gloom of night will stop my fellow mail carriers and me from delivering junk mail.

One day, I delivered an envelope full of coupons to a home that was addressed: "To the Smart Shopper at ..."

The next day, the envelope was returned with this note scrawled on it: **"Not at This Address."**

—VANESSA PEEBLES

Bill Gates and the president of General Motors were having lunch. Gates puffed out his chest and boasted of the innovations his company had made. "If GM had kept up with technology the way Microsoft has, we'd all be driving $25 cars that get 1,000 m.p.g."

"I suppose that's true," the GM exec agreed. "But would you really want your car to crash twice a day?"

We bank tellers receive a lot of sweets as gifts from our customers around the holidays. One morning at breakfast, I was telling my husband that the bank employees had the potential to gain weight on the job. "Yeah," my husband said slyly, "you're all going to turn into 'teller tubbies.'"

—STEPHANIE BURTON

Pulling into my service station 45 minutes late one morning, I shouted to the customers, "I'll turn the pumps on right away!" What I didn't know was that the night crew had left them on all night. By the time I got to the office, most of the cars had filled up and driven off. Only one customer stayed to pay. My heart sank.

Then the customer pulled a wad of cash from his pocket and handed it to me. "We kept passing the money to the last guy," he said. "We figured you'd get here sooner or later."

—JIM NOVAK

My son, Earl, is a construction foreman. One day he tumbled from a scaffold, managing to break his fall by grabbing on to parts of the scaffold on the way down. He received only minor scratches.

Embarrassed by the fall, he climbed back up to continue working. Then he noticed his coworkers holding up hastily made signs reading 9.6, 9.8, and 9.4.

—JANICE A. CRABB

@@@@@@@@@@@@@@@@@@@@@@@@@@@@@@@

As a trail guide in a national park, I ate with the rest of the seasonal staff in a rustic dining hall, where the food left something to be desired. When we were finished with meals, we scraped the remains into a garbage pail and stacked our plates for the dishwasher. One worker, apparently not too happy after his first week on the job, was ahead of me in line. As he slopped an uneaten plate of food into the garbage, I heard him mutter, "Now stay there this time."

—IAN A. WORLEY

My boss at the warehouse told the new guy not to stack boxes more than head-high. "If the inspector shows up," he said, "we'd get in trouble. So, questions?"

"Yeah," said the new guy. "How tall is the inspector?"

—CYNTHIA FRANKLIN

On the door of the post office in rural Esperance, N.Y.:
PULL
If that doesn't work, PUSH.
If that doesn't work, we're closed.
Come again.

—VERA KASSON

While on a business trip, I traveled via commuter train to my various appointments. Before each stop, a petite, fragile-looking conductor entered the car. In a surprisingly booming voice, she clearly and authoritatively announced the destination.

One passenger complimented the conductor on her powerful voice, asking, "How do you manage to speak so forcefully?"

"It's easy," she replied. "I just visualize my kids sitting in the back of the train, doing something they shouldn't."

—JOSEPH FRANCAVILLA

"No, *you* roll over!"

The photo in our local paper showed a cubicle that had been destroyed by a fire. The accompanying article said it happened in a state office building and the blaze started when something fell onto a toaster, accidentally switching it on and igniting some paper.

I was about to turn the page when my husband asked, "Did you notice where it happened?"

"No," I said. "Where?"

"At the Bureau of Occupational and Industrial Safety."

—STEFANIE SWEGER

@@@@@@@@@@@@@@@@@@@@@@@@@@@@@@@@

The woman needed encouragement to keep peddling the exercise bike in her gym. So my friend, the gym manager, said, "Close your eyes and imagine you're riding along Broadway in New York City. It will be more interesting."

Inspired, the woman cycled on, but after a minute she stopped.

"What's wrong?" asked my friend.

"The traffic light's red," she replied.

—JULIA ADIE

My husband took an evening job at a large mortuary. He would arrive at 5 p.m., as most of the staff was leaving, and worked until 10 p.m. greeting visitors. On his second night I decided to call and see how he was doing. A secretary who was working late answered the phone.

"Is Mr. Sloan there?" I asked. I heard papers being shuffled. "I'm sorry," she finally replied. "Mr. Sloan is not ready for viewing yet."

—WILODEAN SLOAN

A farmer called my veterinary office and asked me to make a house call. Because the road was closed, he parked his ancient pickup in a field for me to drive the rest of the way. But once behind the wheel, I realized the brakes didn't work. The truck sped toward the stable, across the farmyard, into the barn, and embedded itself in a gigantic haystack.

Sweating, I climbed out and apologized. "Don't worry," the farmer said to me. "That's how I stop the car, too."

—JOSEPH HOLMES

Working at a major satellite company, I was expecting two technicians from the phone company who were coming by to do repairs. When they arrived, I was surprised to see that both were women. Wanting to appear equally emancipated, I called the only woman in our information-technology department to be their guide.

As we waited for Ellen, I thought about the strides women have made over the years.

When Ellen showed up, she smiled and nodded to the two women. Then she turned to me and said, "So, what happened to the guys from the phone company?"

—VICTORIA TOLINS

Recently, I went to use the ladies' room in the office building where I work. I beat a hasty retreat, however, after seeing this sign inside: "Toilet out of order—please use floor below."

—CLAIRE ROSKIND

World's worst jobs:

- Nuclear Warhead Sensitivity Technician
- Vice President, Screen Door Sales, Reykjavík, Iceland, Division
- Sperm Bank Security Guard
- Road Kill Removal Crew
- Russian Cartographer
- Prison Glee Club President
- Assistant to the Boss's Nephew

—CLUBFUNNY.COM

America's Funniest Jokes, Quotes and Cartoons from Reader's Digest

Laughter, the Best Medicine

More than 600 jokes, gags, and laugh lines. Drawn from one of the most popular features of *Reader's Digest* magazine, this lighthearted collection of jokes, one-liners, and other glimpses of life is just what the doctor ordered.

ISBN 978-0-89577-977-9 • $9.95 paperback

Laughter Really Is the Best Medicine

Guaranteed to put laughter in your day, this side-splitting compilation of jokes and lighthearted glimpses of life is drawn from *Reader's Digest* magazine's most popular humor column. Poking fun at the facts and foibles of daily routines, this little volume is sure to tickle your funny bone.

ISBN 978-1-60652-204-2 • $9.95 paperback

Laughter, the Best Medicine @ Work

A laugh-out-loud collection of jokes, quotes, and quips designed to poke fun at the workplace. Laugh your way through the 9-to-5 grind with this mix of hilarious wisecracks, uproarious one-liners, and outrageous résumés. No matter how bad your day, you'll find that laughter really *is* the best medicine for all your work woes.

ISBN 978-1-60652-479-4 • $9.99 paperback

Laughter, the Best Medicine: Those Lovable Pets

People are funny, but so are the animals we love, and this book brings to life the often entertaining relationships we have with our animals. A chuckle-inducing collection dedicated to the companions we hold so dear—our pets.

ISBN 978-1-60652-357-5 • $9.99 paperback

For more information, visit us at RDTradePublishing.com
E-book editions are also available.

Reader's Digest books can be purchased through retail and online bookstores.
In the United States books are distributed by Penguin Group (USA) Inc.
For more information or to order books, call 1-800-788-6262.